New Orleans

120th anniversary
anniversary
Berlitz

- A ☞ in the text denotes a highly re
- A complete A–Z of practical information starts on p.106
- Extensive mapping on cover flaps

Berlitz Publishing Company, Inc.

Princeton   Mexico City   Dublin   Eschborn   Singapore

Copyright © **1998**, 1995 by Berlitz Publishing Co., Inc.
400 Alexander Park, Princeton, NJ, 08540 USA
9-13 Grosvenor St., London, W1A 3BZ UK

All rights reserved. No part of this book may be reproduced or transmitted in any form or by any means, electronic or mechanical, including photocopying, recording or by any information storage and retrieval system without permission in writing from the publisher.

Berlitz Trademark Reg. U.S. Patent Office and other countries
Marca Registrada

Text:	Ken Bernstein
Editor:	Sarah Hudson
Photography:	Jon Davison, Greater New Orleans Tourist & Convention Commission, New Orleans Historic Voodoo Museum
Layout:	Media Content Marketing, Inc.
Cartography:	Visual Image

Thanks to Mrs. Beverly Gianna of the Greater New Orleans Tourist & Convention Commission for her valuable assistance in the preparation of this guide, and Micheal Tisserand for providing his updated information.

Found an error we should know about? Our editor would be happy to hear from you, and a postcard would do. Although we make every effort to ensure the accuracy of all the information in this book, changes do occur.

ISBN 2-8315-6329-1
Revised 1998 – First Printing March 1998

Printed in Switzerland by Weber SA, Bienne
019/803 REV

CONTENTS

NEW ORLEANS

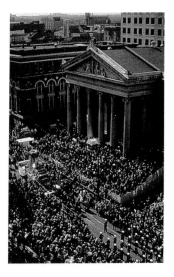

THE CITY AND ITS PEOPLE

Escapism is a fair excuse, if you really need one, to visit America's least typical city. With a temperament floating somewhere between the Deep South, Europe, and the Caribbean, New Orleans manages to remain largely immune to the stresses afflicting other big cities. This crucial but utterly relaxed Mississippi River port, living by its own subtropical priorities, manages to have a whale of a time, incidentally eating rather better than anywhere else this side of Paris.

The City Care Forgot

Whether it's partying or pursuing an offbeat lifestyle, this city of half a million (one and a quarter million in the metropolitan area) looks at life with generosity and tolerance. The easygoing approach to differences—philosophical or racial—is most noticeable in the French Quarter, which has attracted more than its share of artists, nonconformists, hedonists, charlatans, ageing hippies, and other individualists. Even the panhandlers are a notch above the national average as they offer appealing and amusing stories, true or otherwise.

The French Quarter—the Vieux Carré ("Old Square") in French—is the historical and spiritual heart of New Orleans, abutting the Mississippi at its tightest bend. Actually rectangular, the Old Square is a grid of 18th-century urban planning. Its landmarks, adorned with lacy, wrought-iron balconies, are interspersed with all-but-hidden courtyards, and enough hotels, restaurants, and bars to billet and refresh the visiting hordes. Preservationists have spared the district from most of the incursions of "progress," such as neon signs and traffic lights.

Story and song alike have made the Quarter's main street as celebrated as Broadway or Piccadilly. Bourbon Street is

New Orleans is a hotbed for many types of music, but the city is most famous for its Dixieland jazz.

naughty, raucous, and vibrant. catering to every desire or whim and offering so much to see and do that pedestrian throngs tend to gape in amazement and delight, their videos zooming and panning in abandon. The accompanying sound track is terrific, with live jazz on almost every corner. (Rock and roll and louder art forms are drowning out some of the jazz these days, but it's all still first class.)

Beyond the French Quarter grew a city of radically diverse neighbourhoods—a metropolitan area covering nearly 200 square miles (518 sq km), not counting municipal swampland. Just upriver, where the American interlopers first settled, is the Central Business District (known as the

CBD), a high-rise mirage of metropolitan muscle visible from the edge of the bayous.

Keeping all the elegance of the Old South, the Garden District stretches from the CBD to the University District and Audubon Park. Another park, vast by any standard, is City Park, extending nearly to Lake Pontchartrain, the largest lake in Louisiana. In a stirring feat of engineering, it was bridged in 1956; driving across the 39-km (24-mile) causeway makes you feel all at sea.

Creoles and Cajuns

Irish, Italians, Germans, and all kinds of immigrants plunged into the multi-racial melting pot of New Orleans, but the city is best known for two early strains of settlers, the Creoles and the Cajuns. The Creoles were defined as descendants of early French or Spanish colonists (see page 19). Still communicating in French long after the Americans took over, the Creoles consigned the upstart Yankees to the far side of Canal Street. By extension, "Creole" can now refer to anything that goes back to New Orleans traditions.

A city that celebrates as much as New Orleans sometimes needs the police to keep order.

The Creoles also looked down on the Cajuns, French-Canadians who arrived in the 18th century, exiled by the British from Acadia (Nova Scotia). Country folk, fur trappers, and fishermen, the Cajuns still keep many of their customs alive today. In addition, Creole and Cajun

The front of a house on Royul Street in the French Quarter burst forth with patriutism plantlife.

cooking have put New Orleans on the gastronomic map of the world.

New Orleans claims more good restaurants per head than any other American city. Food, from alligator to zucchini, is a preoccupation—just look out for the swarms of locals queueing up to be admitted to somewhere expensive. Also check out any souvenir shop or bookstore, and you'll find stacks of cookery books that are produced locally.

New Orleans also enjoys first-rate bread and coffee, full of character. The chicory-laced café au lait and beignets, fluffy crullers powdered with sugar, make a definitive, heartwarming start to the day—or perhaps a dawn nightcap.

To be frank about the climate, it's hard to avoid mentioning the rain. Statistics by the U.S. Weather Bureau show an average annual rainfall of almost 140 cm (60 inches), making New Orleans the wettest of all the 68 stations reporting. The Mississippi, firmly contained behind massive levees, has become less of a threat to the city now than the rain. Accumulations of rainwater, propelled through 4,000 km (2,500 miles) of tunnels, canals, and pipes, are sucked up by giant screw pumps and deposited in Lake Pontchartrain at a rate of 84,000 cubic metres (3 million cubic feet) per second.

As for the temperature, it's comforting to know that virtually every hotel room is air-conditioned. Don't expect too much pre-dawn relief outside in the summer—the temperature reaches a sticky 20° C (80° F) most mornings. Storms can also add to the discomfort between June and November, possibly bringing tornadoes and even hurricanes.

The most pleasant season is the spring—around the time of Mardi Gras or later—when the temperatures are mild, the rainfall less abundant, and nature at its most optimistic. Winter can be frostier than you think: note the succinct warning

Neutral Ground

Elsewhere they call it the "median strip," or "central reserve," or "traffic safety island"—that strip, often gardened, which separates two roadways. Since the early 19th century, the expression has been "neutral ground" in New Orleans. When the United States bought the Louisiana Territory, the native Creoles didn't want to have anything to do with the invading Americans. The French Quarter stayed French and the newcomers were forced to build houses on the less civilized side of what is now Canal Street. The "neutral ground" separating hostile neighbours made such an impression that all such strips in town, stately or utilitarian, now go by that name.

posted at almost every bridge and viaduct: BRIDGE MAY ICE IN COLD WEATHER. On a sweltering hot summer day it seems somewhat mocking.

Geography Lesson

Many a new arrival to New Orleans has asked "Where's the ocean?" or "Which way to the beach?" The Gulf of Mexico is over 100 miles (160 km) away. Yet New Orleans is one of the world's busiest seaports. Just as evocative as Mark Twain said it was, the surging Mississippi River is eminently navigable, and paddlewheelers, now teeming with tourists, zigzag among the freighters and tankers.

If you're looking for mountains, or even hills, you've come to the wrong place. New Orleans is, as the "politically correct" expression would say, "altitudinally disadvantaged": it lies beneath sea level. Grave-digging was soon found to be impossible, and so above-ground cemeteries grew into imposing Cities of the Dead, the last word in mausoleum architecture, with marble palaces and sculptures for the elite and tiers of coffin-sized lockers for the rest.

Four Virtues?

The most pompous of New Orleans funerary monuments must be the one at the entrance to fashionable Metairie Cemetery (see page 52) marking the tomb of Daniel Moriarty and family. You'll see it from Interstate I-10 on the way into the city.

Late in the 19th century, Moriarty ordered a fitting monument for his late wife—a huge cross and life-sized statues of the Four Virtues. The sculptor said he knew of only three virtues. Moriarty insisted on four, known today to everyone in New Orleans as "Faith, Hope, Charity, and Mrs. Moriarty."

Because of the meandering nature of the river, the normal directions of the compass have to be generally ignored here. There is no "north side" or "east end," but "riverside" or "lakeside," "uptown" or "downtown" instead. In the most awkward example of disorientation, the west bank of the sinuous Mississippi is found directly to the east of the French Quarter. So don't worry if a moment of panic strikes as you drive east over the bridge into the sunrise and see the sign announcing the West Bank Expressway.

A car will come in handy when it's time to explore the surroundings. You'll get a taste of the antebellum South along the river, where Spanish moss trails romantically from huge oak trees and crinolined ladies guide visitors through colonnaded, white plantations. You can head for the bayou country for a boat tour of the swamps, cameras at the ready to capture beaver, deer, turtles, pelicans, and alligators; the bears are usually hiding. You can also tour the clean, green, spacious state capital, Baton Rouge, where the king of southern politicians, Huey Long, ruled and died (see page 31). And don't pass up a trip to Acadiana— Cajun country, with its French-accented fun and festivals, and serious cooking. Even if you miss Mardi Gras (see page 76), there's so much going on—rollicking or simply exotic—that you'll hardly have time for a full night's sleep.

Colourful disguises hide the identities of these festive Mardi Gras revelers.

A BRIEF HISTORY

What, an 18th-century visitor might well have asked, is a nice town like New Orleans doing in a place like this? Below sea level, below river level, hot and sticky in the long summer, surrounded by pestilential swamps, vulnerable to every flood and hurricane, and more than 160 km (100 miles) from the Gulf of Mexico—or anywhere else. All in all, a very odd location for a seaport with ambitions to be an industrial and cultural centre.

More modest goals inspired the native Americans (Choctaws and other Indian tribes) who lived here for thousands of years before the arrival of the French colonists. Their survival course entailed avoiding water snakes and alligators, repelling mosquitoes, and navigating their dugout canoes through the impenetrable bayous. On the plus side, they enjoyed a cornucopia of seafood and game, flavouring it with a hot sauce that the Creoles would adopt with relish.

The first European to sight the Mississippi River was the Spanish Conquistador Hernando de Soto, brother-in-law of Balboa, the discoverer of the Pacific. De Soto's link with the Mississippi turned out to be particularly poignant. When he died of a fever in 1542, his companions consigned him to Old Man River.

The French connection was to begin in 1682 when René Robert Cavelier, Sieur de La Salle, claimed for France a huge swath of territory radiating from the Mississippi. In honour of his king, Louis XIV, he coined the name *Louisiane*. When he returned with a convoy of colonists, to his embarrassment he couldn't find the river's shifting mouth. Therefore, the pioneers ended up in Texas instead, where most perished. Mutineers assassinated La Salle.

Seventeen years later, to rebuff growing English interest in the region, France sent a further expedition, led by Pierre le Moyne, Sieur d'Iberville. He rediscovered the elusive Mississippi, which, until the U.S. Army Corps of Engineers took control two centuries later, changed course at whim.

Iberville and his younger brother, Bienville, established several tentative settlements along the Mississippi, and in 1718 Bienville marked the spot for New Orleans. There were two obvious advantages to the site: its strategic significance, controlling a tight curve in the Mississippi near an alternative waterway, Lake Pontchartrain; and the abundance of food, from shrimp to wild boar. Bienville later served as the first governor of Louisiana, and the brothers are remembered today in the names of two parallel streets in the French Quarter. Bienville also merits a statue outside the train station.

Hanky-Panky by Law

The first con-man in the lurid history of New Orleans was a Scotsman with the reassuring name of John Law. He was a pioneer of the property scam —promoting distant marshland as a paradise. Luckily for New Orleans, he succeeded.

The Mississippi delta is known for its indigenous blues music and unforgiving swamps.

A financier and highroller gambler, on the run from England after a fatal duel, John Law finagled a deal with the French government—a 25-year charter to develop the Louisiana Territory. All he needed were investors and settlers, whom he lured with a propaganda campaign. On posters Law distributed in France, the purported El Dorado was pictured as a prosperous seaport at the foot of a small, totally fictitious mountain. Handsome Indians were portrayed handing over gold to contented colonists.

When Law's clients arrived after wretched months at sea, the truth about the Mississippi Bubble hit them like a tornado. Huts and tents were all there was, and the roads were generally quagmires, but there was nowhere else to go, so the pioneers were forced to pitch in and try to survive.

John Law's promotional activities weren't confined to the gullible French, either. He signed up some 10,000 Germans, mostly Rhinelanders, to share the "golden future" in Louisiana. After ghastly hardships on the way from Germany, via France, to the New World, a small minority of the original group of settlers actually made it to the banks of the Mississippi.

Today, west of New Orleans, along what is called the German Coast, you can see towns with names like Hahnville, Kraemer, and Des Allemands. Most descendants of the Ger-

Casket Girls

Many shortages nagged at the early colonists, but the one they brooded about the most was the absence of female companionship. Governor Bienville appealed to Paris, "Send us some women." The regent Philippe soon obliged, opening the gates for 88 exportable female prisoners. Other shipments brought hundreds more ladies of the streets and other jailbirds as prospective brides. However, the family tree of the French colony also includes some eminently respectable wives. A number of unblemished young middle-class ladies patriotically answered the call to join the colonists. Escorted by Ursuline nuns, they arrived carrying their trousseaus in hope chests, from which they got their name—casket girls. Within a few weeks they were all spoken for.

An irresistible array of fruits and vegetables brightens stalls at the French Market.

man pioneers, however, Frenchified their names: thus Delmaire was originally Edelmeyer and Fauquel was Vogel.

Some of the other early immigrants were less fortunate than the Germans. Black slaves from Africa arrived in the earliest years of the colony. In 1724, the French government enacted the *Code Noir* (Black Code), which regulated slavery and the rights of free blacks. Among the benefits, slaves did not have to work on Sunday. The code, considered more liberal than the laws elsewhere in the South, remained in force in Louisiana for a century. As for John Law's bubble, it burst in 1720 and he died in 1729, a down and out in Venice.

High Society

By the middle of the 18th century, New Orleans had grown into an acceptable town, not exactly self-sufficient but beyond the survival stage. To carry this a step further, a certain tone of French luxury was imported by the Marquis de Vaudreuil (Governor Bienville's successor in 1743), who attempted to transform New Orleans into an overseas Versailles. *A bon vivant* who held extravagant parties, Vaudreuil and his elegant wife presided over a sort of "Golden Age" of social grace, when the colonial elite were invited to plays, musicales, and balls.

On the side, however, the governor and his cronies were busily pocketing bribes, as was the custom in the self-financing French colonial service. He can therefore be considered as the founder of a grand old Louisiana tradition—political corruption. He deserves credit though, as well, for organizing the first system of man-made levees which protect the city from the Mississippi.

In plantation days, before the Civil War, New Orleans surpassed New York in exports.

When Vaudreuil was promoted to Governor of Canada, his successor, the Chevalier de Kerlerec, was left to pick up the pieces, and became the scapegoat when investigators from Paris got round to studying where all the money had gone. Although unskilled in accounting, the Choctaw Indians held Kerlerec in very low regard and nicknamed him "Chef Menteur" ("Chief Liar"). As you drive eastwards from New Orleans along the Chef Menteur Highway, think of the hapless governor.

¡Caramba!

Diplomats love their secrets, so the citizens of *Nouvelle Orléans* were among the last to learn about the 1762 Treaty of Fontainebleau. Overnight, it appeared, they were handed over to King Charles III of Spain. It all made perfect sense to King Louis XV, cousin of Charles (both were Bourbons), for the French and Indian War (known in Europe as the Seven Years War) had pulled the rug out from under France's North American empire. Britain won Canada and everything east of the Mississippi, including Spanish Florida. Louisiana was now isolated in a British-ruled part of the world, a money-losing outpost that seemed to have no future. Louis decided to let Cousin Carlos try to make a go of it.

It came as an almost unbearable shock to the patriotic Frenchmen of New Orleans to be told, a couple of years after the fact, that they were retroactively Spanish citizens. Waiting for the first Spanish governor to arrive put a huge strain on the disillusioned society. When Governor Antonio de Ulloa finally sailed up the Mississippi in 1766, four years after the treaty was signed, a crashing storm erupted, as if an omen for the climate ahead. The governor, a scholarly retired naval officer with good intentions, was accompanied by a contingent of 80 Spanish soldiers, most of retirement age.

What seemed to upset the locals as much as anything was that their new master came supplied with casks of cheap Spanish wine instead of bottles of their habitual Bordeaux.

Memories of high-society frolics of the Vaudreuil era brought bitterness when the Spanish governor's wife froze out the Creole ladies of New Orleans from official invitation lists. French-speaking citizens protested the snub with a petition and a demonstration that got out of control and turned into violence. Spain called it treason. The harrassed Ulloa could take no more and sailed into exile.

The second governor sent from Spain, Lieutenant General Don Alejandro O'Reilly, cracked down on the rebels. He was "doubtless the most able of all Spanish soldiers," the French ambassador noted, adding, "It's a pity he's an Irishman."

O'Reilly created the Cabildo, or town council, and led New Orleans towards prosperity. But he is remembered with bitterness. To make clear the authority of Spain and extinguish dissent, he ordered the execution of five Creole rebels. They went before the firing squad on the Esplanade near where it crosses Frenchmen Street, named in their memory.

The Acadians

During the troubled Spanish era, thousands of French exiles from eastern Canada—Acadians, or Cajuns—migrated to Louisiana. For years their territory had been the target of a struggle between the British and French, and the British victory in the French and Indian War forced them to leave, as they remained fiercely loyal both to France and the Catholic church.

Unlike the other colonists, who eventually melted into the culture that became Louisiana and the United States, the Cajuns kept to themselves in the bayou, retaining their 17th-century language and customs. Only in the 20th century did they

*The memories of Spanish rule in New Orleans are,
at best, bitter-sweet.*

start to communicate in English as well. The present Cajun
population in Louisiana, numbering in the hundreds of thousands, still largely keeps to itself. But one aspect of their culture, a glamorized version of spicy Cajun cooking, has spread
across the United States and, more recently, the world.

The French Quarter

Light a big fire on Good Friday and you'll be stirring super-
stition and legend. In 1788 a Spanish official, lighting a de-
votional candle in the private chapel in his home on Chartres
Street, started a fire which spread, fanned by the wind, to de-
vour nearly half the town.

New Orleans looked on the positive side of the disaster.
Taking note of the obvious vulnerability of the old wooden
houses, the government set up new building standards. Tile
roofs became the rule, and structures with more than a single
floor had to be built of brick. Spanish colonial touches such
as gardened patios, shaded balconies, and adornments of

Stars and Stripes may flutter over Louisiana, but Napoleon's legal system still lingers on in local government.

wrought-iron gave the area its almost Caribbean air. The new town became known as the French Quarter.

Revolutionary Antics

During the American Revolution, New Orleans plunged in on the revolutionist side. It wasn't only enthusiasm for the Yankees; Spain declared war on England in 1779. The governor of New Orleans, 23-year-old Don Bernardo de Gálvez, seized the chance to help the colonists in their struggle against George III, and led raiding parties that kept the far-flung British outposts along the Mississippi on the defensive.

After the American Revolution came the French Revolution, and a new world order. The ambitions of Napoléon Bonaparte stretched as far as the Western Hemisphere. By the secret Treaty of Ildefonso in 1800, France regained Louisiana from Spain. Napoléon thought it was a good idea at the time, as it combined a renewed embrace of the Francophile citizens of New Orleans and a vast expansion in the Western Hemisphere at the expense of his British rivals.

But in 1803, only three years after retaking it, France sold Louisiana to the United States for $15 million. It was a controversially huge fortune at the time—more than the U.S. Treasury owned—but the Louisiana Purchase, reaching from Canada to the Rockies to the Gulf of Mexico, almost doubled the area of the United States. The deal turned out to be the bargain of all time—something like four cents an acre for what became Iowa, Arkansas, Missouri, Nebraska, South Dakota, and the most part of Kansas, Louisiana, and Oklahoma.

As usual, New Orleans was among the last to learn of all these manoeuvres, thanks to the secrecy of diplomatic negotiations and the slow communications of the age. In the event, within one month three different flags flew over the *Plaza de Armas,* also known as *Place d'Armes* (and now Jackson Square). The Stars and Stripes replaced the French flag on 20 December, 1803, only three weeks after Spanish rule officially gave way to French. Once again, the stunned citizens felt abandoned and betrayed.

The Yanks Are Coming!

President Jefferson's choice of governor for the hostile, or at least uneasy, population of the Territory of Orleans seemed, to say the least, inauspicious. William Charles Cole Claiborne was a Protestant from Virginia, aged 28, who needed a brace of interpreters to communicate in both French and Spanish. He judged the Creoles honest but lazy and ill-educated, their town ugly and filthy. His horror at the city's sanitation was understandable; he would lose two wives to yellow fever in New Orleans.

The culture gap was reciprocated. The local Creoles considered themselves more worldly than the rustic Americans;

after all, New Orleans had been dressing up for fancy balls since the middle of the 18th century. In fact, during Claiborne's early days, the style of local dance music caused discord between the Creoles and Americans that escalated into fights in more than one ballroom.

Claiborne persevered, however, learned French, changed the laws, and brought his carping constituents into the American fold as citizens of the new State of Louisiana. Still, it remained nothing like any other U.S. state, with both French and English as official languages. Duelling, although illegal, became a daily passion. Even the governor was unable to avoid getting involved in an "affair of honour" and was actually wounded in a duel with Congressman Daniel Clark. The favourite setting for defending someone's honour was a spot under the great oaks in what is now City Park. The deaths mounted inexorably.

War on the Mississippi

Less than two months after Louisiana won its statehood, the United States went to war with Britain—for the second and last time. To everyone's surprise, New Orleans became the stage for the most glorious, indeed the only, American victory of the whole conflict.

The War of 1812 was fostered by accumulated American grievances over trade restrictions, complaints against British warship commanders who were suspected of shanghaing American sailors off merchant ships, and territorial ambitions. There were dramatic naval battles and a final ghastly defeat for the United States when the British burned down the city of Washington.

Finally, the warring parties focused on New Orleans. A British flotilla, diverted from the Caribbean, sailed up the Mississippi with some 10,000 first-class troops. The Americans rushed Major General Andrew Jackson to New Orleans to command the city's defence. Outmanned and outgunned, Jackson mobilized a force of somewhat irregular members: an unlikely coalition of Tennessee and Kentucky militiamen, local Creoles, free blacks, Choctaws, and associates of the privateers Jean and Pierre Lafitte (see box, below). The pirates may well have been the key to the outcome, for they alone knew the real ins and outs of the bayou country, from where the British attack would come.

In the Battle of Orleans—you can visit the scene along the river in Chalmette—General Sir Edward Packenham and his redcoats, with British drums and bagpipes urging them forward, marched in proper formation across the battlefield like toy soldiers—straight into a meatgrinder of American artillery and small-arms fire. In less than half an hour it was all over: General Packenham, the brother-in-law of the Duke of Wellington (famous for his war successes), had been shot from his horse, thousands of his troops had been killed, and the tattered survivors withdrew in disarray. Packenham's body was later shipped back to England pickled in a barrel of rum.

Freebooters

Jean Lafitte and his brother Pierre ran an empire deep in the bayou country near New Orleans, based on what some called piracy; but the charge was never proven in court. In 1813, Governor Claiborne offered $500 for Jean Lafitte's capture, but the insolent rogue just posted an offer of his own—$1,500 for the capture of Claiborne. In 1814 the two privateers were overcome by patriotism; by volunteering their inside knowledge of the bayou country, they helped General Jackson plan his tactics in the Battle of Orleans against the British (see above).

Afterwards, Jackson won the brothers a full pardon. As for himself, the battle was the key to the White House. "Old Hickory" was elected 7th president of the United States.

The war, in any case, was over. Ironically, it should have been over before the battle was ever fought. A peace treaty had been signed in Belgium two weeks before, but news travelled no faster than a ship in those days.

Between Wars

The sound of prosperity after the war was the blast of steam whistles on the river. With the development of powerful steamboats, navigation on the Mississippi became a practical, economical matter. Freighters moved cotton, tobacco, and sugar downriver and worldwide. Passenger ships like the *Natchez* and the *Belle of Memphis* were palaces with food, drink, music, and romance.

Thousands of steamboats—first sidewheelers, then the more powerful sternwheelers—docked along the quays every year. By 1840 New Orleans was the world's largest cotton port, second only to New York as a general port, and the fourth biggest city in the United States, with a population of 100,000.

There was always something to do in New Orleans. Carnival parades began in 1837, although other aspects of Mardi Gras festivities had taken hold much earlier. The French Opera House, at the corner of Bourbon and Toulouse streets, opened in 1859 and supported the nation's first resident opera company.

On quite another cultural plane, a law against gambling, dated 1798, was almost universally ignored in New Orleans, where the card game of poker is said to have originated. One of the leading lights of card games was Bernard de Marigny, a millionaire playboy. His most memorable contribution was a dice game called craps (from *crapaud*, French for toad) about which he was wild. Laying out Faubourg Marigny, the suburb he built, he named one of the streets

Stern-wheelers still ply the Mississippi at New Orleans, but these days they're just for fun.

Craps Street. The churches on Craps Street protested that there must be a better name, which is why Burgundy Street now extends so far downriver.

It's quite possible that New Orleans owes more to John McDonogh than to any other single benefactor. A plantation owner of Scottish extraction, he educated and freed many slaves. Most of City Park is land he willed to the children of New Orleans. When he died, a millionaire, in 1850 (when a million dollars really meant something), he left his money to the cities of Baltimore and New Orleans to build schools for the poor. Dozens of schools in New Orleans are named after McDonogh, who, in effect, founded the city's public school system. School children collected the coins that paid for the McDonogh Monument erected in 1898 in Lafayette Square.

Surrender

The Civil War brought hardship and pain to the owners of slaves in the city of New Orleans. Less than half of the black population were slaves, and those that were led a less onerous life than in most other parts of the South. "Free people of colour" ran their own businesses and owned property. "Free women of colour" were included among the concubines of white aristocrats, their lives organized according to arcane social codes.

In January 1861, Louisiana joined other cotton states in seceding from Lincoln's Union. After two months as an independent entity, the state entered the new Confederacy, but because of its strategic significance, New Orleans became a high-priority target for the northern military forces.

In April 1862, a Union naval force led by David G. Farragut capitalized on Confederate unpreparedness and penetrated the defences of New Orleans. As a sign of protest, 15,000 bales of cotton were burned at the riverside to keep them from the enemy, and steamboats were set ablaze and floated downstream to harrass the Yankee fleet. Despite this, Farragut came ashore as the conqueror.

Dixieland

All of the southern United States is known as Dixie, or Dixieland, thanks to a lively song by Dan Emmett, who rhymed "cotton" with "forgotten." In 1861 the tune emerged from minstrel shows to become the unofficial anthem of the Confederacy. The origin of the name, though, can be traced to New Orleans. In 1860 the Citizens' Bank of Louisiana issued $10 bills with "TEN" printed on one side and the French equivalent, "DIX," on the other. New Orleans started to be called "Dixie," and the label was soon applied to the whole of the South.

After a week, the American flag was raised over New Orleans. It announced a military occupation which was destined to endure beyond the Civil War into the Reconstruction period for a total of 14 bitter years.

The price of surrender was the presence of General Benjamin Butler, unaffectionately known as "Beast" Butler. With 18,000 occupation troops, the general took over the city, reminding the citizens at every occasion that they had lost the war. Orleanians still recount with indignation the "atrocities" committed by Butler: persecuting local ladies who tried to demoralize his troops, harrassing unsympathetic clergymen, and confiscating family silver for the war effort. To all-round relief, the general was withdrawn less than a year after he arrived, with a reprimand from Abraham Lincoln.

Call to arms — a dealer of antique guns presents an historical specimen of the city's outlaw spirit.

Post-Reconstruction

After the wrenching years of occupation, the actual reconstruction of New Orleans was allowed to begin. Jetties were built in 1879 to speed the flow of the Mississippi near its mouth, improving navigation and returning the port to a position of strength. New railway lines linked the city with the rest of the United States.

In 1884 the city attempted to demonstrate its post-war recovery by staging an international fair—the World's Industrial and Cotton Centennial Exposition. The morale-boosting exercise lost money; much of the fairground, however, was made use of and turned into Audubon Park. Meanwhile, the rest of the United States had started to hear about the industrious but amusing city on the Mississippi as a place worth visiting.

The Storyville Story

Storyville, an X-rated recreational area that could hold its own with Hamburg's Reeperbahn or Bangkok's Patpong, was named, to his embarrassment, after Alderman Sidney Story, a reformer. In 1897 he pushed through an ordinance outlawing prostitution everywhere in the city *except* for a small, specific area just beyond the French Quarter, where it could be contained and controlled.

Storyville became a legend in its own time, where the mixture of glamour, depravity, and colour in the local brothels attracted almost every visiting celebrity, and where saloon drinkers, gamblers, pimps, and rakes waiting their turn could tap their feet to newly developing style of music—jazz.

Soon after he was sprung from the Waifs' Home, Louis Armstrong started playing his bent, nickel-plated cornet in the dives of Storyville. He improvised from evening to daybreak for 15 cents, which was eventually raised to $1.25 a night. His career took a turn for the better when he joined a dance band on a riverboat. Storyville lasted exactly 20 years. In World War I the U.S. Navy Department ordered the creation of a vice-free zone for five miles around every naval base. That included Storyville. United in patriotism, the entrepreneurs left.

The Long Saga

In Louisiana, politics and politicians have always been a fascinating business—and business is the word—but none of the bosses could compare with larger-than-life Huey P. Long (1893–1935). When he was cut down in his prime, 100,000 admirers came to see his open coffin.

Long was cagey, ambitious, poor, and so bright he graduated from Tulane Law School less than a year after he en-

An ancient mini-submarine, used by the Confederacy in Lake Pontchartrain, is on display at the Presbytère.

tered. At the age of 25 he was elected to the state public service commission, where he began to mount populist attacks against the public utilities. As governor he built roads and bridges that were desperately needed and supplied all the state's school children with free textbooks. His slogans were "Every Man a King" and "A Chicken in Every Pot."

Elected to the U.S. Senate, he still controlled Louisiana from Washington, having installed a puppet in the governor's office. The story goes that his rubber-stamp stooge, aptly named O. K. Allen, was so compliant that he once signed a leaf that blew on to his desk. Long was starting to attract a national following when he was assassinated in the state capitol in Baton Rouge on 8 September, 1935.

Huey Long was not the last of the colourful governors. One of his immediate successors, Governor Richard W. Leche, was forced to resign in 1939, caught in a federal corruption crackdown. Sentenced to 10 years in prison, he remarked, "What the hell, it's an occupational hazard."

Towards 2000

After the Second World War new highways led to broader horizons, and suburbs began to sprawl. After the construction of the impressive causeway across Lake Pontchartrain in 1956, commuters even began to move to the far side of the lake, and vast shopping complexes followed them. Other construction fantasies have resulted in the most ambitious project

---

Early Government

Huey Long's rather eccentric brother, Earl, served three times as governor and was elected to Congress just before his death in 1960. As his mental state became more delicate, he was installed in various psychiatric clinics. In one, a state institution, he dismissed the chief administrator and appointed a new one, who promptly released him.

to date: the Louisiana Superdome (see page 92).

New Orleans prospered in the space race as NASA assembled thousands of technicians at suburban Michoud to produce its booster rockets. Desegregation in schools, which hit many southern cities hard in the 1960s, passed off in New Orleans with a minimum of trouble. Whites and blacks had always mixed more freely here than in most places in Dixie, and the drive for racial equality reached an historic high in 1977 when Judge Ernest "Dutch" Morial was elected the first African-American mayor. After two terms in office he was succeeded in a landslide victory by Mayor Sidney J. Barthelemy, also an African-American.

Old and new worlds merge in New Orleans. A modern office building looms behind an historical district.

In recent years new cultural and recreational facilities have multiplied the city's tourist potential. These include greatly expanded riverfront parks, a "state-of-the-art" aquarium, and a cherished French Quarter that seems to get better with age. All this, and the promise of legal gambling afloat and ashore, brings the city's vocation for tourism to the fore.

Nearly three centuries after the intrepid Iberville erected a cross at a crescent in the Mississippi, New Orleans offers more romance than ever.

WHERE TO GO

Finding your way around New Orleans is trickier than in some other American cities. In fact, the only place you're not likely to get lost in is the French Quarter, the Vieux Carré, a logical grid of streets you can explore on foot. Cars tend to traverse the Quarter slowly because of all the stop signs, one-way streets, and confused out-of-town drivers. In addition to this, to preserve the gas-lit atmosphere, there are no traffic lights. Beyond the Quarter stretches the newer city, with former plantations and marshes developed into city blocks and suburbs.

Because of the twistings of the Mississippi, normal directions of north, south, east, and west are inoperative. Downriver lie Faubourg Marigny (a suburb), St. Bernard Parish, and Chalmette, where the Battle of Orleans was fought (see page 25). Upriver, Faubourg Ste-Marie has become the sky-scrapered CBD (Central Business District). Farther uptown, the Garden District runs on into the University District, and, beyond them, Riverbend is a desirable residential area.

Towards Lake Pontchartrain, Mid-City is dedicated to residential housing and the vast City Park.

There are many ways to see New Orleans, but the following three are recommended: a bus tour to get your overall bearings; a do-it-yourself excursion on the St. Charles Avenue streetcar; and a river cruise for an idea of the expanse of the city and the importance of its port.

THE FRENCH QUARTER

☛ Jackson Square

Our survey starts where the New Orleans story began, during the reign of Louis XV of France.

When the original colony was laid out, they reserved this square as the parade ground, the ceremonial centre of New Orleans. Each time a new ruler gained control over Louisiana, the solemn flag-raising took place here in what was known as *Place d'Armes* and later *Plaza de Armas*. Public executions were also a regular occurence. Things are less serious these days, though visiting dignitaries turn up from time to time.

Around the square the delights of tourism bloom: mule-drawn carriages stand by for sightseeing trips; dancers, musicians, magicians, and mime artists entertain the unhurried passersby; and an academy of licensed sidewalk painters

wait for patrons of the arts to buy their scenic canvases or

Street artists of all kinds keep the local colour bright on the four sides of Jackson Square.

on-the-spot portraits. In the square, surrounded by flowers, is a 10-ton **statue** of Andrew Jackson, hero of the 1815 Battle of Orleans (see page 25). As a symbol of victory, the general is raising his hat high, and the horse balances on its rear legs —no mean feat for Clark Mills, the sculptor.

It's a good idea to start your sightseeing in the twin red-brick **Pontalba Buildings** that border the square, even before you've studied the matching elegance of their architecture. In one of them, at 529 St. Ann Street, an inconspicuous tourist information office is run jointly by the Louisiana Tourist Development Commission and the New Orleans Tourist and Convention Commission (see page 126). It is a prime source of literature and maps and, of course, advice on where to go and how to get there.

The Pontalba ensemble was commissioned by Micaela Almonester, Baroness de Pontalba, a fiery local character of the 19th century. Each of the buildings, fronted with cast-iron balconies, had 16 ground-floor shops and 16 apartments above and are said to be the first apartment houses built in the United

The elegant 19th-century Pontalba Buildings.

*Major General Andrew Jackson's statue
before St. Louis Cathedral.*

States. A few doors from the tourist office you can visit the
1850s House, a recreation of one of the Pontalba apartments
with furnishings of the time. The other apartments, still considered most desirable dwellings, are actually lived in.

The father of Micaela Almonester, a self-made Spanish
grandee named Don Andrés Almonester y Roxas, was the
force behind the building of **St. Louis Cathedral**, the oldest
active cathedral in the country, which dominates the square.
There had been a church on the site since 1727, but it burned
down in the Good Friday fire of 1788 (see page 21). When
the new church was dedicated as a cathedral in 1794, Almonester was given a permanent seat of honour and a Spanish
knighthood; he is buried in the crypt.

In the Presbytère are faces of old New Orleans.

The present cathedral, with its slender French-style towers, dates back to the mid-19th century. Free guided tours of the minor basilica point out the fine stained-glass windows, murals, and statues. Church and state were well provided for on either side of the cathedral. The **Presbytère**, to the right, was originally intended as the rectory, but it served as a courthouse. The **Cabildo**, to the left, was the seat of government, where the documents of the 1803 Louisiana Purchase (see page 23) were signed. In 1988 the Cabildo suffered serious damage in a fire. Both buildings are part of the Louisiana State Museum, whose exhibits include Napoléon's death mask (a gift from Bonaparte's doctor) and relics from the Battle of Orleans (see page 25).

In the arcade of the Presbytère is displayed an ancient mini-submarine, which used to be touted as the Confederacy's first iron submarine, scuttled in Lake Pontchartrain. A new plaque says its origin is in doubt.

On the Waterfront

The Mississippi is not only extremely wide, but also so deep at its crescent curve in New Orleans that ocean-going vessels can tie up right alongside the shore, minus piers or pillars. This is the most navigable part of the whole 3,780-km (2,350-mile) length of the river—its depth is more than 60 metres (190 feet).

The first levees here were Nature's own high banks that were built up by the river's currents. Engineers heightened and strengthened them to protect the low-lying land from inundation. During the 20th century, security was assured

The Cabildo , the former seat of French government in New Orleans, was damaged by fire in 1988.

The Moon Walk Pavilion is a fine vantage point for watching the nautical action on the New Orleans waterfront.

by sturdier dikes, a network of pumping stations, and more miles of canals than Venice.

You can see the levees, and stroll along them. Just across the road from Jackson Square, **Washington Artillery Park** is a popular vantage point: in one direction are the spires of the cathedral and the atmosphere of the Vieux Carré, in the other is Old Man River, nearly half a mile wide at this point.

Moon Walk, a delightful promenade by the river, follows the bend for a close view of the nautical action, which includes giant container ships, old-fashioned freighters, tug-propelled barges, and sternwheeler cruise ships.

Moon Walk gets its name from the nickname of a fondly remembered mayor, Maurice Landrieu, who was in office in the 1970s when the landscaping took place. Just upriver you can see the Crescent City Connection, the collective name of a pair of bridges linking New Orleans with the West Bank (which just happens to be due east at that point).

Until relatively recent times the riverfront here was strictly utilitarian, with freighter piers, warehouses, and anything else to discourage the tourists. One of the buildings blocking the river view from Decatur Street was the century-old **Jackson Brewery**, where the local Jax beer was brewed. The location became too valuable for industrial use, so the complex was taken apart and put together again as a shopping and recreational complex. There are winning views from its restaurants and bars.

Café du Monde—a New Orleans institution since 1860—serves up scrumptious beignets and chicory-flavoured coffee.

Between the brewery and the wharf runs the **Riverfront Streetcar,** inaugurated in 1988. It deploys vintage electric rail vehicles for the convenience of tourists. The trams, mostly about 70 years old but beautifully renovated, slowly cover a route of nearly 3 km (2 miles) between the Esplanade in the east and the Convention Center in the west. Painted bright red with gold trim, the streetcars are known locally as the "Ladies in Red."

At the Toulouse Street wharf, the steamboat *Natchez* summons prospective passengers aboard using a steam-powered calliope. This and other paddle-wheelers, historic originals or authentic copies, ply the river with a variety of tours, specializing in everything from plantations to the battlefield where the red-coats were wiped out in the final battle of the War of 1812 (see page 24).

The 24-hour-a-day **Café du Monde** has been an institution since the 1860s. More than just a people-watching outpost, this café serves up all the most typical New Orleans pick-me-ups: *café au lait* (half chicory coffee, half hot milk) and *beignets* (pronounced "ben-yay"), puffy crullers dusted in sugar—don't sneeze while you're eating!

The Café du Monde occupies a corner of the Old Butcher's Market, founded in 1813, one of several buildings making up the **French Market**. This is where Choctaw Indian women squatted to sell food and handicrafts to the earliest colonists. Aside from the contemporary shopping—everything from baby clothes to stuffed alligators, pralines to posters—the market is full of history, local colour, and gastronomic opportunities. Jazz is often performed *al fresco*, or you can challenge a blindfolded street chess master to a fast game ($5). Here, too, is an office of the National Parks Service, offering free walking tours of the French Quarter and the Garden District and information about Jean Lafitte National Park.

The **Farmers' Market**, the next part of the old commercial sprawl, makes an art of fresh fruit and vegetables; have tomatoes ever looked so ripe, or chains of garlic so alluring? And it all goes on round the clock. The **Flea Market**, beyond, may be worth a survey for its souvenirs, hand-made jewellery, and bric-à-brac. Incidentally, the locally made voodoo dolls cost more than the forgeries from China.

From here it's only a few steps to the **Old U.S. Mint**, an appropriately grandiose building at 400 Esplanade Avenue. Built during the presidency of Andrew Jackson, this institution produced U.S. coins worth nearly a staggering $300 billion before and after the Civil War.

The ground floor has exhibits on the minting process; upstairs are two divisions of the Louisiana State Museum. The **Mardi Gras** section displays paintings, photographs, costumes, masks, sceptres, and crowns illustrating the history of the New Orleans festival. The **Jazz Collection** provides a short history of the musical form that started in Storyville (see page 30), told through documents, photographs, the actual instruments played by the jazz greats—and music coming out of the walls.

Old New Orleans

The **Old Ursuline Convent** at 1112 Chartres Street is one of the oldest buildings in New Orleans. The original Ursuline nuns here, who arrived in the French colony in 1727, moved

---

Birthplace of Jazz

The jazz pioneered in New Orleans by Louis Armstrong, Jelly Roll Morton, Kid Oliver, and other immortals evolved from a mixture of cultures. The city echoed with Caribbean and African rhythms, arias sung by the opera-loving Creoles, tunes of the military bands and quadrilles, and the uninhibited music of Mardi Gras. The first generation of jazzmen couldn't read music, but how they could improvise!

When the Storyville red light district (see page 30) was closed down in 1917, the world's first and best jazz musicians hit the road bound for Chicago, New York, and Europe. Wherever you hear Dixieland today, it's an echo of Old New Orleans.

You can go back to the roots of jazz in Preservation Hall (see page 47) and some of the Bourbon Street spots or, better yet, in neighbourhood hangouts. Or look in the newspaper listings under Funerals. If the announcement mentions jazz, check out the joyous send-off for the dearly beloved—a marching band in the oldest tradition, the highest tribute from New Orleans.

into this building in 1749. It was the first convent in what became the United States, the first orphanage, the first pharmacy, and so on. The "casket girls" sent over from Paris for arranged marriages with the early settlers (see page 16) were chaperoned here, and the building underwent a further drastic change of character between 1831 and 1834 when the Louisiana State Legislature met here.

Across the street from the convent, **Beauregard-Keyes House** had a very distinguished lodger just after the Civil War: the defeated Confederate general P.G.T. Beauregard. The other half of the name refers to the author Frances Parkinson Keyes (rhymes with "eyes"). Best remembered for the mystery novel *Dinner at Antoine's*, she fortunately took over the house in the 1940s, saving it from destruction. Today there are tours of the elegant Greek Revival townhouse.

The Beauregard-Keyes House, named for its two best-known residents.

Another noble dwelling, the **Gallier House** at 1132 Royal Street, now owned by Tulane University, was both designed and lived in by the architect James Gallier, Jr. It brims with new (for the 1850s) ideas and gadgets— hot and cold running water, ventilation ducts, and an English (instead of French)

garden. Visitors waiting for guided tours of the house can take advantage of a good tea-room on the premises.

At the corner of Royal and Governor Nicholls streets, visitors on guided walking tours of the French Quarter nervously survey the city's best known haunted house, officially **LaLaurie House**. It seems the hostess, Madame Delphine LaLaurie, amused herself by torturing her slaves. In 1834 neighbours fighting a fire in the house discovered seven slaves chained up in the attic. Madame LaLaurie only narrowly escaped a lynching and fled, reportedly to Europe. The ghosts of the seven have been groaning upstairs at midnight ever since.

The Cornstalk Fence has out-lived the Royal Street house it originally encompassed.

In the 900 block of Royal Street, stop to admire the **Cornstalk Fence**, a cast-iron grill with gilt touches depicting cornstalks and morning-glory vines. It was shipped by sea from Philadelphia in 1850. The house behind it burned down, to be replaced by a Greek-Revival mansion, now a small hotel.

A fictional allusion goes to explain the name of **Madame John's Legacy**, a Caribbean-style house at 632 Dumaine Street which may possibly date from 1726. George Washington Cable wrote a story about a local Creole bachelor who willed a house like this to his faithful octoroon (one-eighth black) mistress. Whatever the real story, it's a very old house, possibly the oldest in town and is now owned and preserved by the Louisiana State Museum.

At 724 Dumaine Street, the privately run **New Orleans Historic Voodoo Museum** displays amulets and magical herbs, and a pair of pythons used in rituals. There are no demonstrations of voodoo, but knowledgeable guides take visitors all through the museum, the occult room, and the altar room, explaining the ancient African religion and its influence in present-day New Orleans. In the museum's gift shop you can pick up a *gris-gris* bag to keep bad luck at bay.

Bourbon and More

Something's always going on in **Bourbon Street**, where the unhurried crowds soak up the delights in a playground designed for grown-ups. Named after the noble French family and not the beverage, Bourbon Street has the monopoly on neon flash in the French Quarter; the other streets are more soberly romantic.

Preservation Hall is famous for its Dixieland jazz.

Glaring signs, importuning touts, and the sound of music hint at the pleasures that can be found here. Most of the attractions are, relatively speaking, good clean fun. The street itself is a stage: a team of tap dancers work for coins, a pickup band competes with the more institutionalized jazz and rock, and mime artists use their skilled body language to coax contributions.

Bourbon Street perks up before lunchtime in spite of its hangover and stays lively even into the wee hours when the party's over but the die-hards are deciding where to go for a nightcap. The street is even popular at working people's breakfast time, when bartenders hose down the street and sweepers gather up the night's excesses. "Volunteered" by the sheriff, the sweepers wear T-shirts proclaiming "Orleans Parish Prison"—and never seem to try to escape.

Not many people drift to Bourbon Street for its historical interest, but if you insist, there's **Lafitte's Blacksmith Shop**, a distinguished but deceptive name for a neighbourhood bar. According to a local legend, this rather dilapidated premises in the 900 block was run by the Lafitte brothers (see page 25) as a front for their pirate activities.

Another monument of the Quarter, **Preservation Hall**, just off Bourbon Street in St. Peter Street, dates from the beginning of the 19th century, though its fame as a sanctuary of jazz goes back only to the 1960s. The antithesis of glitzy commercialism, this one-time stable building is the spot for pristine traditional Dixieland jazz performed by veterans who play the old classics from the heart.

Bourbon Street is remarkably well endowed with Old Absinthe Houses. Two bars lay claim to the title, in a dispute going back to the speakeasy days of Prohibition. French tradition called for water to be added drop by drop before absinthe could be consumed, and a lavish marble "drip fountain" ended up in the newer of the Old Absinthe House bars. The drink has long since been banned because of its addictive properties; the amazing change of colour when it is diluted can now be demonstrated using alternative anise-flavoured products.

One of many architectural examples of regal elegance that define Royal Street.

Hermann-Grima House, at 820 St. Louis Street, is a mansion built in 1831 by a prosperous businessman from Germany, Samuel Hermann. When Hermann went bankrupt, the house was taken over by his lawyer, Felix Grima. Incorporating elements of colonial French and Spanish and Georgian styles of architecture, it now belongs to the Christian Women's Exchange, who run it as a museum and more. The authentic old kitchen is used for demonstrations of Creole cooking and the spacious patio is a very fashionable venue for cocktail parties.

For a painless survey of local history and legends, you can tour the **Musée Conti**, 917 Conti Street, a wax museum portraying notables from the explorer La Salle to the incumbent governor of Louisiana. The stories behind some of the displays are rather racy, so the guides give a special, less scandalous commentary to school groups. Most of the lifelike wax images were made in Paris— the hair is Italian and the eyes German glass.

At the turn of the 19th century the power of Creole finance was concentrated at the intersection of Conti and Royal streets. A bank stood on each corner. **Royal Street** still lives up to its name, with many of the buildings being models of regal elegance. Among the highlights in a single block are the Old Louisiana State Bank (number 401) with its fine wrought-iron balcony; Casa Faurie (number 417), now Brennan's Restaurant, built in 1801 for a rich merchant; and the Auguste Coudreau Mansion (number 427) with filigreed, double-decker, cast-iron galleries. Across the street, the Civil Courts Building, which has filled an entire block since 1908, has been a favourite set for visiting film companies. The Historic New Orleans Collection (number 533) has exhibits on local history for the public and a glorious private library, open only to researchers. In addition to all the above, Royal Street is also the headquarters of the city's best art galleries and antiques shops.

Chartres Street (pronounced "Charter" in modern-day New Orleans), is noted for its fine mansions, shops, and restaurants. A curious historical landmark is **Napoleon House** (number 500), built at the end of the 18th century. It belonged to Nicholas Girod, the mayor of New Orleans, who conceived a plot to rescue Napoléon Bonaparte from exile on the island of St. Helena. This house was actually expanded to provide a new base for the emperor, but he died before any of Girod's dreams could be realized. Now it's a bar full of atmosphere, where people from around the world come to wash down a bit of history with a Pimm's Cup or a Sazerac (see page 103).

At 514 Chartres Street, the **New Orleans Pharmacy Museum** was the apothecary shop of Louis J. Dufilho, Jr.,

America's first licensed pharmacist. The classic apothecary jars contain all kinds of voodoo potions along with more conventional medicines. The stronger of heart can also take a closer look at leech cures and surgical instruments dating from the mid-19th century.

All over the French Quarter, aptly shaped Lucky Dog hotdog vans can be found. Notwithstanding the magnificent cuisine available in the Quarter's restaurants, it seems that there are sufficient fast-food appetites to keep all these mobile units busy.

THE FRINGES

The once-fortified boundary of the French Quarter, **Rampart Street**, has the urban blues. Most of the buildings along the street are decaying, and visitors are advised not to wander here after dark. The same warning applies to **Louis Armstrong Park**, honouring New Orleans' best known hero. The park is notorious for muggings—except when crowds gather for performances at the Municipal Auditorium or the Theatre for Performing Arts.

The same danger signals emanate from the **St. Louis Cemetery**, the oldest of the "cities of the dead" in New Orleans. Don't go exploring among the historic tombs unless you're part of a group. The most visited tomb here belongs to Marie Laveau, the Voodoo Queen who exercised an electrifying and sometimes terrifying influence over all levels of New Orleans society for much of the 19th century. Notice the freshly added voodoo charms and symbols.

Another Rampart Street landmark is **Our Lady of Guadalupe Chapel**, built in 1826. It was sited strategically near the cemeteries, to afford efficient send-offs for epidemic victims. Four saints occupy niches of honour in the rear: St. Martha, St. Martin de Porres, St. Joseph, and St. Expedite. St.

Expedite? Legend has it that the crate containing the statue arrived with no identification except for the label, "Expedite!" Behold, devout New Orleans proclaimed a new saint.

The widest business street in New Orleans, **Canal Street**, dividing the French Quarter from the Business District to its west, follows the long, straight trajectory of a canal that never got off the drawing board. In the beginning of

Lucky Dog hot dog stands are a familiar source of fast food in the French Quarter.

the American era here, Canal Street was a barrier between the Creoles and the gringos, the "neutral ground."

Toward the river along this busiest of shopping streets, one whole block is occupied by an historic building, the **Old Customs House**. It's even bigger than it looks. When completed, far behind schedule, at the end of the 19th century, it was considered the largest federal building in the United States except for the Capitol in Washington. Inside, see the stupendous marble hall at the top of the ceremonial stairway, lined by 14 Corinthian columns. When the Yankees took over New Orleans during the Civil War, the Customs House became a military prison and the headquarters of the despised General Benjamin Butler (see page 29).

Foreign consulates and international firms occupy many of the offices in the 33-storey **World Trade Center** at the river end of Canal Street. At the summit is a revolving bar, the **Top of the Mart**, which seats 500 and is open until midnight

(2:00 A.M. on Saturday). The view is ever-changing as the lounge makes one revolution every 90 minutes. Because of

Gravely Majestic

The spooky problem arose in the earliest days of the French colony of how to bury the dead in a place so marshy that a coffin would float to the surface in the first rainstorm. The answer in below-sea-level New Orleans was above-ground interment. It was a chance for rich and prominent citizens to employ the best architects and stonemasons, leaving no neo-classical stone unsculpted, to create mausoleums rivalling the most pompous European models. For the poor there were tiers of vaults in the wall, irreverently called "ovens." Many generations wind up in the same box, the older remains being swept to the rear.

The metropolitan area has 42 cemeteries. The most spectacular for architecture is Metairie Cemetery. Notable, too, is St. Louis Cemetery number 3, on Esplanade Avenue, on the tour bus itinerary. Save Our Cemeteries Inc offers guided tours of Lafayette Cemetery number 1, tel. 588-9357.

the prevalence of cocktails it is off limits to children, who can be served a non-alcoholic view on the floor below.

The **Plaza de España**, a tiled square on the riverside that is reminiscent of Spain, leads to the ticket booths of river sightseeing trips and to the work-a-day **Canal Street Ferry**. This is the cheapest boat trip on the Mississippi—free for pedestrians—and it takes less than 10 minutes one way, barring traffic jams on the river. On the opposite shore is **Algiers**, a district of the New Orleans municipality, but far removed in atmosphere from the city center across the river.

The thousands-strong cast of characters at the **Aquarium of the Americas**, on the riverfront at the end of Canal Street, can be as delightful as penguins, as disquieting as alligators. The exhibitions focus on North and South America, with particular emphasis on the Mississippi River, nearby swamps and bayous, and the Gulf of Mexico. The Gulf contingent, drifting around a 1.5 million-litre (400,000-gallon) fishbowl, includes sharks, tarpon, and stingrays. Tours on the John James Audubon Riverboat combine all this with a river tour and a stop at the Audubon Zoo (see page 61).

On the opposite side of Plaza de España begins the long, thin shopping mall called **Riverwalk**, dedicated mostly to non-essentials and things you never knew you needed. Among the 200 shops are food halls offering varied delights, and souvenirs both corny and unique. It's all air-conditioned, with river views. Beyond Riverwalk is the **Convention Center**, named in honour of Ernest "Dutch" Morial, the city's first African-American mayor (see page 33). When New Orleans is hosting a convention large enough to occupy the centre's entire 65,000 square metres (700,000 square feet), you can hardly escape the ramifications. Even so, the Center is being expanded.

Inland from the Convention Centre, **Piazza d'Italia** is a curious post-modern ensemble surrounding a pool in the shape of Italy. It is dedicated to the city's large Italian-American contingent, whose culture, food, and drink captivate all of New Orleans around the time of Columbus Day. Other plazas with overseas connections are nearby. **British Place** features a statue of a bulldog-like Sir Winston Churchill, and a magnificent gold-plated equestrian statue of Joan of Arc occupies the **Place de France**, between the World Trade Center and Rivergate.

The **Warehouse District** has had its ups and downs, but several of its semi-derelict buildings have recently been gentrified and it's now considered a desirable address.

Algiers Point

Some might say the best thing about Algiers is the view back across the river to the skyline of New Orleans. The district does have a certain charm, however, and the sleepy air of a small Mississippi river town whose house-proud citizens near the port spruce up their gingerbread houses.

Every ferry is met by a minibus from **Blaine Kern's Mardi Gras World**, a unique tourist attraction. Calling itself the "largest float-building firm in the world" (you can have your very own festive vehicle made for only $125,000), the establishment supplies New Orleans with most of its Mardi Gras masks, props, and figures.

Its works have also been seen at other festivities, from the Mummers Parade in Philadelphia to Bastille Day in Cannes. Dozens of designers, artists, sculptors, and craftsmen work here year-round, but it gets a little hectic just before Mardi Gras.

The Aquarium of the Americas houses thousands of aquatic animals, including albino alligators (inset).

Many of the warehouses have been transformed into art galleries and artisans' workshops. For art fans, antiques collectors, and students of urban redevelopment, the area, which is centred around Julia Street, has its idiosyncratic appeal.

If you have youngsters in tow, the **Louisiana Children's Museum** at 428 Julia Street should be high on your list of places to go. Here the kids have fun while learning skills and tricks—blowing enormous bubbles, staging a TV show, shopping in a make-believe supermarket, toying with gravity, and using computers.

A few blocks away, the Louisiana Historical Association operates the **Confederate Museum** in a curious, gloomy

A monument on the move: the St. Charles streetcar links the CBD and the Garden District.

Romanesque-style building at 929 Camp Street. Most of the exhibits were donated by survivors of Civil War veterans. The widow of Jefferson Davis (the only President of the Confederate States of America) donated her husband's top hat and walking stick, inkstand, paperweight, and binoculars. The hall is full of battle flags, guns of all calibres, uniforms, and medals, and the shop sells books and prints as well as "genuine Confederate money and bonds."

THE CBD

Thanks to the lie of the land you can see the **CBD**, as the **Central Business District** is abbreviated, from miles away. The utter flatness of the surroundings magnifies the high-rise effect. The 51-storey One Shell Square building holds the local altitude record, closely followed by some of the new skyscraper hotels. As the CBD has evolved in fits and starts, reasonably historic Beaux-Arts fantasies are still interspersed with modern glass-and-steel workhorses. An ambitious and modern complex with lawns and sculptures, the **Civic Center** encompasses City Hall, the State Supreme Court Building, and the State Office Building, as well as the well-stocked municipal library. Nearby, the 1950s Union Passenger Terminal concentrates its efforts on intercity train and bus traffic. Distin-

The Central Business District, known locally as the CBD, lights up a New Orleans night.

guishing the main concourse are charming murals packed with details of New Orleans life.

It would be difficult to miss the **Louisiana Superdome**, a vast, superlative-packed stadium that looks like a spaceship in repose—or the world's biggest mushroom. Twenty-seven storeys high, it can seat 75,000 for a football match (even more for a concert) under its 3.6-hectare (9-acre) dome. Political and sports fans as well as anyone interested in engineering or architecture will enjoy one of the 45-minute guided tours of everything from the press room to the locker room. Note that the seats, with their clever colour scheme, are arranged in a deliberately irregular way so that TV cameras panning the audience make the house look permanently full. Plans are afoot to construct another arena nearby to accommodate hockey, basketball, and boxing.

The **New Orleans Centre** (the English spelling is considered stylish) is a modern shopping mall with some big-name department stores and boutiques under an atrium. It adjoins the vast Hyatt Hotel, with over 1,000 rooms.

☞ THE GARDEN DISTRICT

Given the cold-shoulder by the French Quarter, the Americans who settled in New Orleans after the Louisiana Purchase (see page 23) chose a convenient, leafy place to build

Shotguns

In many parts of New Orleans the most popular style of architecture was and is the shotgun house.

It's not known whether anyone tried it, but the name implies the firing of a single shot through the front door to come out the back without hitting an internal wall. This style of long narrow house with the rooms all in a row became popular because under French law only the width of a dwelling was taxed.

A shotgun variation, the "camelback" house, has a small narrow front which expands into a two-storey section in the rear; another way to fool the taxman.

their mansions, in what is now called the Garden District. Getting to it can be a sightseeing adventure all of its own — the St. Charles streetcar line is a national historic landmark and a bargain, at $1 each way.

Founded in 1835, the streetcar line that opened up the Garden District to commuter development runs some 21 km (13 miles) from the centre of town out to the former suburb of Carrollton. The present rolling stock, though thoroughly overhauled since, dates back to the 1920s. The first and last stop in the Central Business District en route for the Garden District is at the corner of Canal Street and Carondelet.

One of the first sights on the way to the Garden District is **Lafayette Square**, the early American answer to the French colony main plaza (now called Jackson Square). Among the monuments to admire in Lafayette Square is a statue of John McDonogh, the benefactor of the public school system (see page 27). Facing the square, the early Americans' city hall was **Gallier Hall**, still a stately example of Greek-Revival architecture.

The tram continues along St. Charles Avenue past Julia Street to **Lee Circle**, a gardened traffic roundabout from which rises a giant, marble plinth supporting a magnificent bronze statue of General Robert E. Lee.

Just beyond the circle, and before the expressway overpass, the modern K&B Plaza office building manages to contribute more than its share to urban culture with an outdoor sculpture gallery. Works by sculptors such as Henry Moore, George Segal, and Isamu Noguchi loll about the plaza.

The streets intersecting St. Charles Avenue beyond the freeway have elegant, classical names which are all in accordance with the plans of the 19th-century developer of the Lower Garden District. They celebrate Greek muses such as

Terpsichore, Thalia, and Melpomene (but pardon the local pronunciation). A sign of the times is Martin Luther King, Jr., Boulevard, which runs as the lakeside portion of Melpomene Street.

Sumptuous homes in plantation style, and also Italianate or Gothic-Revival style, make this is a neighbourhood for roaming in and admiring at leisure. The most interesting homes are just off the St. Charles Avenue streetcar line in parallel Prytania Street (another allusion to ancient Greece) and its intersecting streets from First to Fourth streets. Here the settlers were out to impress the neighbours, and they surely succeeded. Unlike the Creoles in the French Quarter, whose houses abutted the street and faced inward around a central patio, the Americans built their mansions set back from the street behind iron fences, gardens, and lawns. The oldest house in the district is thought to be the plantation model in Federal style at 2340 Prytania Street, built around 1838. It is described as a "Louisiana raised cottage," but if that suggests a small, simple house, don't be fooled.

Tulane University, located on St. Charles Avenue, is strong in law and medicine.

In the 6300 and 6400 blocks of St. Charles Avenue, two renowned universities rub shoulders. **Tulane University** was given its present name in 1883 when businessman Paul Tulane donated a million dollars. The university is strongest on medicine, law, and the arts and sciences. Right next door, **Loyola Univer-**

sity is the biggest Roman-Catholic college in the South. The Jesuits run this co-educational institution, best known for its law school.

Audubon Park, across St. Charles Avenue from the universities, reaches all the way to the river. From unspectacular beginnings (see page 30), it's dedicated today to all kinds of recreational activities—golf, tennis, jogging, cycling, fishing, and rollerskating, not to mention picnicking under the great oak trees. The 138-hectare (340-acre) park is named after John James Audubon, an American naturalist and artist who spent a fair amount of time in New Orleans teaching drawing. He would go to the French Market (see page 42) to buy birds that had been shot by hunters in order to study their anatomy.

The highly rated **Audubon Zoo** has many instructive services, but it's also fun. There are camel and elephant rides, animals that children can pet, and the usual cast starring lions, tigers, and monkeys. For local colour, visit the section with alligators and other features of Louisiana swamp life.

CITY PARK

An equestrian statue of a local hero, General Pierre Gustave Toutant Beauregard, who ordered the Confederate attack on Fort Sumter that started the Civil War, stands guard at the main entrance to **City Park**. By any standard this is truly a whopper of a park—over 600 hectares (1,500 acres) of gracefully landscaped recreation. City life seems far away in the midst of blazing crepe myrtles and avenues of live oak from which the Spanish moss seems to weep.

This former plantation now provides facilities for golfers, horseback riders, baseball and football players, fishermen, sailors, hikers, and joggers. An art museum and a botanical garden provide less physically taxing diversions.

Audubon Park is a haven for recreation, including golf, tennis, fishing, and picnicking.

For a touch of history, see the **Duelling Oaks**, where early-19th-century Creoles settled affairs of honour (see page 24). You might say this was the headquarters of the greatest swordsman of the age, José (Pepe) Llulla, an immigrant from Spain's Balearic Islands. He fought many duels, won them all, died of old age, and was buried in a cemetery he conveniently owned.

Children enjoy City Park's **Storyland**, complete with its fairy-tale theme, and the adjoining amusement park which offers excitement aboard the roller-coaster and Ferris wheel. For small children and adults, the highlight may be the Last Carousel, a classic merry-go-round which is nearly a century old and has splendidly restored wooden horses, giraffes, and other enchanting animals.

The park's **Botanical Garden**, a project designed to provide work during the 1930s Great Depression, includes

fountains, statues, and indoor and outdoor flora collections
—ferns, orchids, palms, and lilies.

Nearest the main entrance to City Park, an airy Neo-
classical building is home to the **New Orleans Museum of
Art**, filled with surprises: pre-Columbian art, Dutch Mas-
ters, and Fabergé eggs. Because of the city's historical
French connection, NOMA has collected artists such as Pi-
casso, Braque, and Dufy, but a special place of honour goes
to a portrait painted by Edgar Degas when he visited some
of his relatives in New Orleans. Touring exhibitions also
stop here. The museum is open from Tuesday to Sunday,
10:00 A.M. to 5:00 P.M.

Just southeast of the main park entrance, along Bayou St.
John, the Louisiana Landmarks Society operates **Pitot House**,
named after an early New Orleans mayor, as a museum. This
18th-century plantation house, the only one in town open to
the public, is furnished with period antiques from Louisiana
and other states. At 1440 Moss Street, the museum opens from
Wednesday to Saturday only from 10:00 A.M. to 3:00 P.M.

LAKESIDE

City Park's northern boundary approaches but doesn't quite
reach **Lake Pontchartrain**, a sizeable recreational advantage that's now more appreciated than ever. The lake is so
big it's disorientating: when you approach New Orleans by
air, it's like coming in to land over the sea. The lake's area is
over 1,600 square km (600 square miles), far smaller than
any of the Great Lakes but mightily impressive owing to the
very flat surroundings, which seem to magnify its size.
Pontchartain's tides are temperamental because it is so shal-
low, with a depth ranging from 3 to 5 metres (10 to 16 feet).

Lakeshore Drive follows the southern shore of the lake
for 9 km (5½ miles) from Lakefront Airport (small aircraft

only) to West End Park and its pleasure boats and seafood restaurants. Along the drive, built on reclaimed land, you'll see luxurious houses as well as picnic grounds and other facilities. The Mardi Gras Fountains produce multicoloured special effects.

Although yachts, fishing boats, and windsurfers abound, the catch about Lake Pontchartrain is that the brackish water is not recommended for swimming, though efforts are underway to restore the lake to its former, unpolluted state.

For all the superlatives attributed to the lake, the one most recognized is man-made. It's the **Lake Pontchartrain Causeway**, the longest bridge of its kind in the world, built across the lake in 1957 and stretching a lengthy 38 km (24 miles) from Jefferson Parish to St. Tammany Parish. Traffic was heavy enough to justify construction of a parallel span a decade later. It's a lonely experience driving across it.

The southern end of the causeway lands in **Metairie**, a suburb best known for its historic cemetery and shopping mall. Something special in Metairie is **Longue Vue** House and Gardens, subtitled "a grand city estat," surrounded by 3 hectares (8 acres) of spectacular gardens. From the stately alley of oak trees leading to the mansion's front door, the house looks like a 20th-century version of a plantation house, situated just across the city line from New Orleans. Impeccably furnished with English and American antiques, Longue Vue was built on the eve of World War II by New Orleans cotton tycoon Edgar B. Stern and his wife.

DAYTRIPS

Plantations

For the flavour of the Old South, take a day excursion or drive yourself to plantation country. Bordering the Mississippi levees all the way from the outskirts of the metropolitan area west to Baton Rouge, these elegant old houses are open to visitors. As often as not, the guide who'll show you around is a softly spoken lady in a hoop skirt.

These columned mansions, most of them built by skilled slaves, were specially designed to withstand the climate, and to proclaim the wealth of the planters in their Neo-classical architecture, furnishings, and attention to detail.

Here is a checklist of eight plantations, starting just downriver from New Orleans and going upriver towards Baton Rouge (see cover for a map). Most are close to the Mississippi, reached by rural roads which follow both banks and collectively are known as the Great River Road. (The scenery on the way isn't always thrilling, due to the industrial sprawl and the height of the levees, cutting off river views.) Visiting hours are usually from 9:00 or 10:00 A.M. to 4:00 or 5:00 P.M. every day of the week, except major holidays. Some of the plantations have restaurants, shops, and overnight accommodation. For further details try the New Orleans Tourist and Convention Commission (see page 126).

Beauregard House

Closest to New Orleans of the plantations here, this relatively simple mansion in the Chalmette National Historical Park is where the Battle of Orleans was fought (see page 25). Doric columns support spacious galleries at both the front and rear. The Beauregard after whom the house was named was the son of the defeated Confederate general (see page 44). Inside are historical exhibits about the War of 1812.

Destrehan Manor

There's a hint of the West Indies in the high-peaked roof of this late-18th-century mansion. Among the house guests

San Francisco House, a shining example of the 1850s architectural style known as Steamboat Gothic.

here were the Duc d'Orléans (the future King Louis Philippe I) and the privateer Jean Lafitte. During the Civil War, the occupying forces turned the property into a hostel for freed slaves. Long abandoned, the house was given over to the River Road Historical Society in 1972, and today it sparkles.

San Francisco

The river, and industry, have moved so close to this charming house that some of the romance has dwindled. But the 1850s architecture, from Neo-classical to Victorian—familiarly known as Steamboat Gothic—is still a treat, and the interiors are most impressive.

 ### Oak Alley

Built in the 1830s, Oak Alley is the quintessential plantation house—a wildly photogenic symbol of the Old South. Visitors arrive with a view of the back of the house, imposing enough, but it's the tunnel of 28 live oaks (all a century older than the house) in front of the columned mansion that really touches the heart. The only authentic effect missing is Spanish moss; one owner hated the stuff and had the trees treated. The Civil War bypassed Oak Alley, which is now run by a non-profit foundation.

Tezcuco

Although it sounds Mexican (the name is said to be Aztec) the atmosphere is more French colonial. The house, of "raised cottage" design, is bigger than it looks. It was built just before the Civil War of cypress and home-made brick. The side galleries are adorned with cast-iron frills.

Houmas House

A classic Southern mansion, the house takes its name from the Houmas Indians, who once lived hereabouts. Begun in the 1840s, the symmetrical Greek-Revival house was once the headquarters of a vast 8,000-hectare (20,000-acre) sugar plantation; but the shifting river has since deprived it of 2.4 hectares (6 acres). Its remarkable interior features in

The interior of San Francisco House is every bit as impressive as its outward appearance.

particular a slender spiral staircase. Outside are twin *garçonnières*.

Madewood

"Queen of the Bayou," this is the only plantation house on our list that's away from the Mississippi; actually, it's near the Bayou Lafourche at Napoleonville. Six stately Ionic columns announce the façade in front; every detail is graceful and symmetrical. The family's slaves are said to have made 600,000 bricks to build the place. The furnishings, though not the original complement, are perfectly appropriate.

Oak Alley is the quintessential plantation house, a wildly photogenic symbol of the Old South.

Nottoway

This stupendous 64-room mansion survived the Civil War thanks to the intervention of a Northern officer who had been a pre-war house guest. Today it's owned by an Australian. The Grand White Ballroom is stunning, and the details, right down to the hand-painted Dresden door-knobs, are impeccable. The only problem is the river, which has moved much closer to the front door than was ever intended.

Swamp Tours

Now that everyone is eco-logy-minded, the sultry

swamps of Louisiana have acquired a new aura of glamour. It's fashionable to observe but not disturb the wetlands wildlife while soaking up the natural history and folklore, rich in stories of Indians, pirates, and Cajuns. There are guided tours of swamp and bayou country from New Orleans, beginning by bus and continuing in a canoe or pontoon boat.

Tourists are rarely eaten, either by alligators or mosquitoes. The sluggish but moving water of the bayous is no place to lay eggs, so the mosquitoes are more likely to live in town. As for the 'gators, they have to be coaxed to even approach the boats—but if you want a close-up view, a food handout goes a long way to help them overcome their shyness.

Among the other fauna visible in or around the river, swamp, and bayou are water snakes, turtles, noisy frogs, and leaping fish, as well as heron, ibis, and majestic egrets. Giant cypress trees thrive in and out of the water, and cypress "knees" rise like stalagmites. All-embracing water hyacinths spread in seemingly epidemic proportions, and along the bayous and steamy backwaters roam wild boar, deer, otter, beaver, and, it is said, even black bears.

Antebellum High-Tech

Inevitably, some of the plantations have stories that are good for business. But the southern belles who take visitors around cover more than legends. They explain the way of life—the airy main house surrounded by galleries, the separate *garçonnière* for the young men of the family, and the slave quarters. They also point out the technological achievements of the age: huge, decorative water cisterns, plate-warmers, fire-screens that convert into end-tables, fly-catching devices, and floor-level mirrors in which milady could check that no ankles were visible.

Some tours will cap the day with a plantation stop or a Cajun meal, music, and dancing.

FARTHER AFIELD

Cajun Country

Since the 18th century, the Cajuns (Acadians) have contributed spice, good humour, and individuality to Louisiana life. Hounded from Canada by the British, the old French colonists of Nova Scotia wound up in the bayou country west of New Orleans as farmers, trappers, and fun-lovers. You can tour the towns and villages that bear the Cajun stamp, hear their old French dialect, eat their suddenly fashionable food, and let your hair down at a *fais do-do*, as the Cajuns call a rousing country dance party. (In French, *fais do-do* is what the children do when

Take a swamp tour to observe the wetlands wildlife while soaking up the local folklore and natural history.

you go out on the town; "go to sleep.")

The capital of Cajun country is **Lafayette**, a city of close 100,000 people. It's less than 2 hours by car from New Orleans on the I-10 expressway; more scenically, take the U.S. 90 route, switching to the more leisurely and interesting State Route 182 beyond Morgan City. Vaunting its French connection, Lafayette posts bilingual street signs (thus West Main Street is also known as *Rue Principale Ouest*). The unusual, modern parish (county) courthouse is also labelled *Maison de Cour, Paroisse de Lafayette*.

The spice of life—a friendly Cajun serves up a feast of fresh crayfish.

Across the street, a colourful old brick building that was once the city hall now belongs to CODOFIL, the Council for the Development of French in Louisiana, an agency struggling against the use of the English language.

Also in Old Lafayette, the **Lafayette Museum** at 1122 Lafayette Street puts local traditions and culture under one historic roof. Beside St. John Cathedral, a Romanesque/Byzantine church built in 1912, stands the **Cathedral Oak**, a 400-year-old tree.

Vermilionville, a kind of Cajun/Creole theme park, occupies a very roomy site along Bayou Vermilion, opposite the airport. Ethnic arts and crafts, music, and food traditions are kept alive here, amongst historic buildings, with plenty of audience participation.

A smaller enterprise designed to recreate 19th-century Cajun society is the **Acadian Village** (West Broussard Road off State Highway 93), which calls itself a folk-life museum. While entertaining and educating the public, Acadian Village employs and trains handicapped people. A Missionary Museum, on the Village grounds, has a collection of Mississippi Valley Indian artefacts, notably a 400-year-old dugout canoe.

Along the road eastwards from Lafayette to the village of **Breaux Bridge**, you'll see old-fashioned oil-well pumps bobbing in the fields. Hereabouts, oil makes the world go round, though the focus has shifted offshore. Breaux Bridge, best known for its annual crawfish festival, is well endowed with seafood restaurants. Fans of Cajun

In Louisiana swamps the giant cypress trees thrive in and out of the murky water.

cuisine are offered three different kinds of hot sauce on every table.

Parts of the downtown district of **St. Martinville** look like a Wild West movie set. Flags of five nations fly in the grand main square in front of the **Presbytère** (rectory), which incidentally, looks like a plantation house. Next door, the 19th-century **St. Martin de Tours Catholic church** traces its history back to 1765.

Right on the edge of town, the Evangeline Oak is supposed to be the tree under which the heroine of Longfellow's Acadian saga, *Evangeline*, met her long-lost lover again. The park surrounding it is dedicated to all the Acadian exiles (see page 20).

New Iberia is known more or less worldwide, for its name appears on the label of every bottle of Tabasco sauce. They run free tours of the factory, on Avery Island. Another industry here is salt mining, but the most interesting family outing is to **Jungle Gardens**, a nature reserve. You can walk or drive through the gardens, which feature a hundred varieties of azalea and up to 1,000 varieties of camellia. Meditate at the feet of a 12th-century Buddha, or alongside the lagoon where alligators coyly wait until you are looking the other way, then climb ashore. Have a look at Bird City too, a sort of Hong Kong of herons and egrets, so popular a nesting place that the inhabitants barely have any room to stretch their wings.

In the centre of the city of New Iberia, a Greek-Revival plantation house romantically called **Shadows on the Teche**, and dating back to 1834, is open for visits. In Weeks Street at St. Peter Street is something even older, preserved behind glass— a white marble statue of the Roman emperor Hadrian, bigger than life-size, said to have been sculpted during his lifetime (second century A.D.).

Baton Rouge

Ever on the lookout for a superlative, Baton Rouge (pronounced "batten") residents are proud to tell you that Louisiana's state capital is the 40th biggest city in the United States, and the petrochemical centre of the world. It's a spacious, placid, very Southern city that moves as slowly as a barge on the Mississippi.

It was in Baton Rouge that Huey Long, the wheeler-dealer governor (see page 31), built the nation's tallest **state capitol building**, reminiscent of New York's Woolworth skyscraper but topped with a lighthouse. Inside, no expense was spared, from imported marble floors and walls to the one-ton bronze doors. From the 27th-floor **observation gallery**, the view to the east covers the Mississippi and the levees protecting the city. Note the dirt factory along the riverbank, where Mississippi riverbed mud is reconstituted into fertile topsoil.

Free tours of the state capitol building always stop at the spot in the back hall where Huey Long was murdered in 1935 (see page 32). In a particularly feverish case of overkill, his bodyguards expended 61 bullets on the alleged assassin. Long is buried in the middle of the spacious lawns and gardens, and his statue faces the capitol he built. The **Old State Capitol**, downriver, is also remarkable—a cast-iron Gothic fortress from the mid-19th century. A gala circular staircase leads up from the rotunda towards a stained glass dome.

A few blocks east, the **Old Governor's Mansion** is not all that old; Huey Long built it, based on the original plans by Thomas Jefferson for the White House in Washington. It's now the Louisiana Arts and Science Center. The *new* **Governor's Mansion**, on a hill in the northern part of the city, is a 40-room imitation of a grand plantation house.

Baton Rouge is the fourth busiest port in the United States. For a close look at the facilities and activities, take a one-hour cruise aboard the sternwheeler *Samuel Clemens*; it departs from Florida Street.

You can tour the **U.S.S. Kidd**, a restored Navy destroyer which fought in many battles in World War II and the Korean War. Its keel and propellors are visible at low tide, and you'll learn more about the ship, along with Naval and Mississippi River history, in the small nautical museum ashore.

Oil and Water

Two unusual monuments sum up **Morgan City**, population about 15,000, on the Atchafalaya River midway between New Orleans and Lafayette along Route 90.

The Spirit of *Morgan City* is an actual shrimp boat, now stranded in the middle of the highway, reminding travellers that

this is the "Jumbo Shrimp Capital of the World."

Nearby, an eternal flame coming from a miniature derrick, commemorates the world's first oil well drilled out of sight of land, in 1947; the Gulf rig was built here, as well as offshore oil platforms used worldwide. Now you know why the local holiday is called the Shrimp and Petroleum Festival.

WHAT TO DO

MARDI GRAS

The madness of Mardi Gras, finale of the Carnival season, overwhelms New Orleans in an irresistible whirlpool of parades, parties, music, fireworks, and all-out merriment.

Although there are an impressive 25,000 hotel rooms in New Orleans, accommodation becomes very scarce as the crucial weekend nears, so you'll have to plan ahead. The biggest event of the year can come at any time between 3 February and 9 March, depending on the moon. It's a moveable feast, pegged to the lunar determination of the date of Easter, but fortunately there is plenty of advance notice. For

During Mardi Gras members of local krewes become deities for the day, throwing trinkets to crowds as they pass.

your immediate calendar: the 1998 Mardi Gras is 29 February; 1999— 16 February; 2000—7 March.

Carnival (from the Latin *carnelevare*, loosely translated as "farewell to the flesh") lasts from the 12th day of Christmas —Epiphany—until what the English piously call Shrove Tuesday; in French it's *Mardi Gras* (Fat Tuesday). The last gasp of hedonism before Ash Wednesday and the meatless penitence of Lent has always been a happy milestone, but New Orleans has made it a riot of fun. Most of the local population, like the invading tourists, are swept up in the non-stop festivities, but a certain percentage of New Orleanians find it altogether too exhausting and make a point of heading for holidays far away at this time.

Since 1837, when the first torch-lit Mardi Gras parade wound through the streets of New Orleans, important tradi-

---

Carnivalingo

Mardi Gras has its own special vocabulary.

Boeuf gras: Fatted bovine, old French symbol of the final pre-lenten dinner, now a giant papier-mâché figure on a float.

Doubloons: Aluminium or plastic coins specially minted by various krewes (see below) as souvenirs.

King cake: Sugar-coated pastry containing a tiny plastic doll. Whoever finds the baby in his portion must buy the next cake.

Krewe: A carnival society, a non-profit club that organizes balls, parades, etc.

Mardi Gras Indians: African-American groups garbed in elaborate feather costumes.

Zulu, Rex, Bacchus, Endymion: Names of major krewes.

Throws: Plastic beads, doubloons, and other trinkets thrown to the spectators.

The streets of the French Quarter are flooded with an endless procession of partiers during Mardi Gras.

tions have evolved. A civic leader dressed as a medieval Rex, the King of Carnival, has presided since 1872.

The krewes (see page 77) still tend to operate like secret societies, uniting people with similar interests, such as businessmen or doctors. New Orleans shakers share membership in the snobbish krewes, barred to ordinary citizens and tourists (unless they have close local contacts). The high-society aspect still carries weight, but a recent—and controversial—local ordinance has banned all krewes from discriminating on the basis of race, gender, religion, or sexual preference.

A revolutionary milestone was the foundation in 1969 of Bacchus, a group with bigger and better floats and, acting as king, a nationally known celebrity instead of an influential civic leader. A newer krewe, Endymion, takes over the Superdome for its fancy-dress ball. Tourists are unlikely to gain entry to any of the big parties except those of Bacchus and Endymion. Huey Long never got invited, either.

Large parades are banned from the French Quarter, due to fire risk, but that doesn't preclude a non-stop street party. And the big parades — Canal Street is your best vantage point — take place from the Wednesday before Mardi Gras until the masquerades of the final Tuesday. The papers have details.

ENTERTAINMENT

New Orleans has always been one of the most entertaining cities anywhere, even in the early colonial days when comforts were few. A visitor in 1804, Major Amos Stoddard, remarked on the "native vivacity of the Louisianians . . . their passion for social intercourse, which is always gratified when opportunities permit. They are particularly attached to the exercise of dancing, and carry it to an incredible excess."

The fun never seems to stop. New Orleans is a no-holds-barred city — the concept of closing time doesn't exist.

Shaken, Not Stirred

New Orleans takes credit for inventing the concept of the cocktail—as well as the very word. In 1793, history tells us, the Royal Street pharmacist Antoine Peychaud concocted a brandy-based brew to pep up favoured clients. It was served in an egg cup, known in French as a *coquetier*. The Americans pronounced it "cocktail," and *voilà!*

The first cocktail to have survived into modern times is the Sazerac, also a New Orleans original. The recipe is bourbon and bitters, the glass having been lubricated with *pastis* (substituting for *absinthe*, which is now illegal). Another local speciality, the Ramos fizz, contains gin, cream, egg-white, soda, and orange flower water. The Hurricane, invented at Pat O'Brien's piano bar, is a compound of fruit juices laced with rum.

The visiting Major Stoddard also noticed a "fondness for games of hazard," reporting that the New Orleans folk of the early 19th century "escape from the ballroom to cards, from cards to billiards, from billiards to dice, and from dice back again to the ballroom." In 1991, the Louisiana legislature legalized riverboat and dockside gambling casinos. Four casino riverboats (and a land-based casino) now operate.

Nightlife

Bourbon Street isn't quite the centre of the world, but it's the natural place to start sampling New Orleans nightlife. There's a bit of everything here—jazz, rock, blues, and nightspots with adult entertainment that's topless, bottomless—anything that you could imagine, and more. A liberal amount of drinking goes on here both day and night among celebrants who sit, stand, or stroll. Americans are notoriously mobile, but you will never see such drinking-on-the-move as on Bourbon Street. Drinking on the street from a bottle or can is illegal, but plastic soon solves that problem— in fine weather the street is overflowing with imbibers slurping down Hurricanes, Daiquiris, or beer from plastic mugs.

The jazz scene in New Orleans is renowned throughout the world.

The Jazz Scene

No drinking at all takes place at Preservation Hall, a sanctuary of Dixieland **jazz** round the corner from Bourbon Street on St. Peter Street (see page 47). It has an interesting way of charging entry—donations are collected at the door.

A selection of less spartan jazz spots in the French Quarter are the *Palm Court Jazz Café*, 1204 Decatur Street; the *544 Club*, 544 Bourbon Street; and *Maxwell Toulouse Cabaret*, 615 Toulouse Street.

Elsewhere, memorable jazz is available at *Pete Fountain's* at the Poydras Street Hilton—expensive

Brass bands blow a big, big sound, spreading joy through the streets of New Orleans.

but impeccable. Just offshore, live jazz is also featured on moonlight cruises aboard riverboats.

Cajun music—foot-stamping country tunes accompanied by a violin, an accordion, and a washboard—can be experienced at *Cajun Cabin*, 501 Bourbon Street; beyond the French Quarter at *Michaul's*, 701 Magazine Street in the CBD; and at *Mulate's Cajun Restaurant*, 201 Julia Street, Warehouse District.

Some other music spots much appreciated by locals are *Tipitina's*, 501 Napoleon Avenue, Uptown, with anything

Other Festivals and Special Events

January: The Sugar Bowl Classic, a big-time college football game with pageantry and many other sports events on the side. The Carnival season officially starts 6 January.

March: The Black Heritage Festival honours the contribution of black culture to Louisiana. St. Patrick's Day brings out marching bands and Irish good cheer. St. Joseph's Day is the Italian equivalent, with parades and food tastings.

April-May: History is exalted in the French Quarter Festival, also emphasizing the local cuisine. For marathoners, the Crescent City Classic is a popular 10,000-metre race. The New Orleans Jazz & Heritage Festival mobilizes local musicians, cooks, and artisans for 10 days. The Greek Festival, yet another ethnic event, shows off music, dancing, and food.

June: The Reggae Riddums Festival features top African and Caribbean musicians and artisans. Motor racing takes over the Central Business District for the Grand Prix du Mardi Gras. The French Market Tomato Festival salutes the ripe red crop with tastings and music.

July: Carnival Latino brings out Caribbean and Hispanic music and food.

October: Locals of German descent and fun-lovers in general join to celebrate Oktoberfest; beer is available. Festa d'Italia takes over the Piazza d'Italia to celebrate the Italian contribution to New Orleans and the world. Gumbo Festival, across the river in Bridge City, exalts the Creole soup/stew. Meanwhile, the Swamp Festival features Cajun music and food.

December: A celebration in the Oaks illuminates City Park with nearly a million sparkling lights. Yuletide traditions from candles to carols are perpetuated in Creole Christmas. New Year's Eve is an excuse for yet another street party.

from jazz to rhythm and blues; *Maple Leaf Bar*, 8316 Oak Street, Uptown, for blues, Cajun, or brass-band music; and *Snug Harbor*, 626 Frenchmen Street, Faubourg Marigny, for contemporary jazz. Across the river in Gretna, *Mudbug's Saloon*, called the world's largest honky-tonk, specializes in big-name country music personalities, but Cajun and rock and roll also feature.

Raucous or intimate bars are another popular aspect of the New Orleans scene. Romantic piano bars are found in some hotels and in the French Quarter at, notably, *Lafitte's Blacksmith Shop*, 941 Bourbon Street. *Pat O'Brien's*, a sprawling bar complex at 718 St. Peter Street, has sing-along piano fun. Bars where gays congregate are mainly concentrated downriver from Jackson Square and in the suburb of Faubourg Marigny.

A musical theme park, "Jazzland," scheduled to open by the year 2000, will offer a wide variety of live music and regional cuisine.

Other Entertainment

Jazz and Cajun music, though immensely popular, have no monopoly on the local cultural scene. Serious **classical music** is dispensed by the Louisiana Philharmonic Orchestra, based at the Orpheum Theater. Visiting artists perform on stages ranging from the Louisiana Superdome (see page 92) to the Municipal Auditorium. Recitals also sometimes take place in churches.

Although the city now lacks an **opera** house, the New Orleans Opera Asociation presents several operas each season at the Mahalia Jackson Theatre of the Performing Arts. The same venue is home to performances of **ballet** under the aegis of the New Orleans City Ballet. Several local **theatre** companies offer contemporary and unusual experimental works. Visiting companies perform Broadway musicals and other big productions.

Three giveaway magazines, *Offbeat, Where,* and *Gambit,* run a listing of entertainment events. Another reliable source is the entertainment calendar which is published daily in the *Times-Picayune,* and a futher source is its Friday leisure supplement, called *Lagniappe.*

SHOPPING

Many visitors come to New Orleans with serious shopping in mind. They've come to the right place, as The Big Easy meets all the requirements and has some distinct advantages.

There's a wide choice of shopping at chain stores as stylish as Saks Fifth Avenue and Lord & Taylor. For strictly local products, shopping areas in various parts of town suggest souvenirs, foodstuffs, or works of art to remind you of your trip. Service will always be courteous and friendly.

Louisiana is also the first American state to offer tax-free shopping to visitors from abroad; in the predominantly surcharge-soaked environment of New Orleans, it's a truly triumphant feeling to be reimbursed for something.

Shops are generally open from 10:00 A.M. to 5:30 or 6:00 P.M. Monday to Saturday. Some, as in the French Quarter, are open on Sundays as well. Shopping malls and French Quarter souvenir shops stay open until 9:00 or 10:00 P.M. daily.

Where To Shop

You'll probably start in the French Quarter, where window-shopping is part of the pleasure of sightseeing. The French Quarter is full of quirky little shops catering for all tastes, from T-shirts, witty or bawdy, to stunning antiques. For particular purchases, Bourbon Street brims with souvenir shops, Royal Street is the most impressive place to peruse antiques. And another stretch rich in both antiques and art is Magazine Street (from the French *magasin*, meaning "store"), which leads all the way from the edge of the Central Business District to Audubon Zoo. The Warehouse District is also dotted with art galleries and antiquarians.

Along the riverfront on the edge of the French Quarter, the French Market (see page 42) has a concentration of souvenir shops, good local restaurants, the local flea market and, for your picnic, or merely to admire, a world-class fruit and vegetable market. A few blocks upriver, the historic Jax brewery between Decatur Street and the levee has been

A French Quarter antiques shop offers everything from Tiffany lamps to chandeliers.

transformed into a shopping mall with more than 75 boutiques, cafés, and restaurants. Yet another style of riverside shopping, the half-mile-long Riverwalk offers an impressive 140 stores and a big food centre. Canal Place, at the river end of Canal Street, calls itself a "fashion mall," with big names like Ralph Lauren, Gucci, and Laroche among the 60 stores and cafés.

Canal Street, the widest street, is the traditional main thoroughfare, on which every kind of store can be found. The prime department store, Maison Blanche, founded in 1897, is still there, with branches in the suburban shopping centres. Still in the Central Business District: the new New Orleans Centre, near the Superdome, has two department stores—Macy's and Lord & Taylor—and three floors of boutiques around a glass atrium.

Bric-a-brac abounds at Le Garage, a popular shop on Decatur Street.

Tax-Free Shopping

It's a bit complicated, but it works. Louisiana Tax Free Shopping (LTFS) gives international visitors refunds for the state sales tax. Now for the small print:

Every shop participating in the scheme has a "Louisiana TAX FREE Shopping" sign at the door. Some malls, like Riverwalk and Canal Place, are tax free zones where every eligible shop is enrolled in the plan. To be eligible for a refund you have to show a valid foreign passport and a round-trip international travel ticket. Resident aliens are ineligible.

Post-modern architecture heralds a mall crammed with everything you could need — Riverwalk.

When you buy something you plan to take home with you, show your passport and ask for a tax refund voucher. You'll be charged the same tax as everybody else, but along with the receipt you'll be given a voucher for the sales tax to be refunded. Don't lose any of the receipts or vouchers.

The LTFS refund centre is located at New Orleans International Airport. Present your receipts and vouchers, your passport, and your air ticket. If your refund is less than $500 you'll be given cash on the spot. Beyond $500 you'll be sent a cheque. You'll be charged a handling fee that ranges from $1 for items costing less than $50, up to $75. If you're in too big a hurry to use the airport refund centre you can do it by mail. For all the details, and a directory of cooperating outlets, ask any tourist information office (see page 126) for a copy of the Tax Free Shopping brochure.

What to Buy

Antiques

New Orleans is remarkably endowed with antiques stores, and not just specialists in the Old South. There are also European, Asian, and African antiques on offer, some of the items so old and interesting you'd expect to find them in a museum. One shop in Royal Street specializes in Civil War swords and antebellum duelling pistols. Others are treasure houses of English furniture, French clocks, Oriental rugs, and antique jewellery.

Arts and Crafts

In addition to old paintings and sculpture, many antiques shops also offer contemporary works by regional artists and artisans. Look for paintings of French Quarter scenes, plantation houses, and the bayou, and bright, original textiles, sculpture, and jewellery.

Specialists sell photographs and prints from all over, as well as American Indian and Eskimo crafts. If you need a portrait in a hurry, go no farther than Jackson Square (see page 34), where a swarm of street artists holds forth.

Books

New Orleans has always attracted artists and writers, and books by and about them abound. Bookstores also have a wide range of other local-interest books—touristic, historical, or photographic. And there seems to be no limit to the ingenuity of New Orleans cookbook writers, who fill the shelves with books promising to educate, amuse, and stim-

The Carriageway Gallery on Royal Street offers a typical selection of works by regional artists.

ulate visiting gourmets with the secrets of Creole and Cajun cooking.

Clothing and Shoes

Thanks to imaginative, relaxed designs and uninhibited colour schemes, American fashion has recruited enthusiasts far beyond its borders. Resort wear, safari styles, casual and comfortable clothing, as well as more elegant garments provide plenty of discoveries. Look over the leisure shoes, as well; there's a wide variety from moccasins to hiking boots.

Food

Marketing experts have outdone themselves in devising gastronomic souvenirs of New Orleans, from small bottles of hot sauce and dehydrated beignet mix to chicory-laced coffee grind. Several firms are geared to ship gift packages of foodstuffs. Bayou To Go, a shop at the airport, can supply departing passengers with packs of fresh or frozen shrimp, crawfish, alligator meat, or sausages. And don't forget the famous pralines (an extra-rich confection of pecan nuts and cane sugar), fudges, and chocolates.

Jewellery

Squads of local artisans produce original jewellery as well as modern interpretations of classical themes. You can buy diamonds loose or set, and also find shops frankly dedicated to counterfeit diamonds and copies of legendary designs.

An array of masks for your Mardi Gras disguise.

Mardi Gras Souvenirs

All year round you can buy masks (suitable for wearing to a party or hanging on a wall), costumes, headgear, sceptres, costume jewellery, "throws," and other paraphernalia of the New Orleans Carnival season.

Music

Immersed in the home of jazz, record collectors can hardly resist stocking up on musical souvenirs of the golden age. All the great names are represented in

local record shops. Broaden your horizons with avant-garde New Orleans jazz, and foot-tapping Cajun and Zydeco music (Zydeco is a black bayou blues variation on Cajun).

Pralines, a confectionary delicacy developed in New Orleans, make a great gift.

Toys and Dolls

New Orleans is the place to pick up a petticoated antebellum doll representing the Old South, or meticulously detailed toy soldiers. Puppets, dolls' houses, games, and toys, either educational or fiendishly distracting, all wait to charm you.

Other Souvenirs

Baseball caps, cowboy hats, Panama hats, posters, or an even more striking trophy for your den, an alligators jaws, can be found all over. The bigger alligators come from the wild, while juniors grow on farms. You can buy a small bag of alligator teeth, minus the open jaws, for just a couple of dollars. Or why not try out voodoo charms and potions on your friends back home? If all ideas fail, T-shirt emporia are everywhere; there are more ways of saying you've been to New Orleans—funny, silly, or merely tasteless—than you'd have thought possible.

SPORTS

From American football to horse-racing in historic surroundings, visiting sports fans can look forward to a varied, exciting menu in New Orleans. There is also one big advantage: it's never too cold for outdoor sports. Summer heat, though, should make you think twice about scheduling; it's advisable to make your active sports appointments very early in the morning or late in the afternoon, before or after the merciless sun has scorched everything in sight.

Participation Sports

On the do-it-yourself side, the possibilities include **golf, tennis, fishing,** and **boating**. And if you're a **jogger**, save some breath for the experience along the Mississippi, on top of the levee that keeps the city dry. For **boating, sailboarding,** and **waterskiing**, Lake Pontchartrain provides a big and frisky challenge. But lake **swimming** is not recommended, because the water tends to be brackish. **Bicycles** may be hired at various locations around town, and you can ride for miles without even seeing a hill.

The two grand municipal parks, **Audubon Park** and **City Park**, are crammed with facilities for a variety of sports. City Park has four 18-hole **golf** courses, as well as a double-decker driving range big enough to entertain 100 players at a time. You can also go **canoeing** among the park's lagoons and **fishing** along its stocked streams or have a game on one of its **tennis** courts.

If you have a liking for history and stately oak trees with your **golf**, play at Audubon Park has been operating since 1895. The scenic **jogging** track in the park is also particularly well thought out, as is the **tennis** court complex. For **horseback riding**, consult Cascade Stables in Audubon Park.

Spectator Sports

Each year the **Louisiana Superdome**, the world's largest indoor stadium, brings several sports spectaculars to the centre of New Orleans.

American Football

In the Superdome you may have the chance to witness a football game involving the local professionals, the Saints—usually on Sunday afternoons; or perhaps, on a Saturday, you can see a college game played by Tulane University. The Bayou Classic is an end-of-season game between Southern and Grambling universities, taking place there in November. On New Year's Day, after a week of sporting events, the Sugar Bowl College Football Classic is played in the Superdome.

Golf in Audubon Park is an historic tradition that goes back to 1895.

Most important of all, the do-or-die climax of the professional football season, the Super Bowl, has been played in the Superdome more often than anywhere else. Even if you're not a fan of American football, the colour and atmosphere of an important game is irresistibly attractive.

For the time being, the Superdome is also the venue for the Sugar Bowl Basketball Tournament as well as significant boxing matches, though a new arena to host such events is planned.

Baseball

New Orleans no longer fields a major league baseball team but the minor league New Orleans Zephyrs are worth watching at the new Zephyr Stadium in East Jefferson.

Horse-racing

Horses have been racing in New Orleans since early colonial days. In 1872 the action moved to the Fair Grounds track, still a nationally known venue for thoroughbred racing in autumn and winter.

Motor Racing

Since 1991, prototypes have been racing in the New Orleans Grand Prix du Mardi Gras, sanctioned by the International Motorsports Association. It all happens over three days in June, on a 2.4 km (1½-mile) circuit downtown.

Ice Hockey

The New Orleans Brass minor-league hockey team hosts games at the recently renovated New Orleans Municipal Auditorium.

The Superdome, home of the New Orleans Saints, has hosted the Super Bowl more often than any other arena.

EATING OUT

Like the French and the Chinese, New Orleanians are wild about food. They go out to eat as often as they can afford, linger over dinner, exchange recipe tips, and read the restaurant critics in the press.

Two piquant cuisines have brought New Orleans its gastronomic fame. Creole, a blend of French, Spanish, Caribbean, and African influences, runs to sophisticated sauces. A bayou offshoot, Cajun cooking has developed a very spicy, upmarket version, now copied far and wide. Both styles capitalize on enviable raw materials, particularly fresh Louisiana seafood.

Where To Eat

Whether your meal consists of classic French cuisine by flickering candlelight or a neon-lit hamburger in a diner, in New Orleans there's a grand choice of cuisine, atmosphere, and price. Many restaurants, including some of the more swanky ones, have relatively inexpensive lunch menus; the portions may be smaller and the recipes less elaborate than in the evening, but it's a good way to survey the gourmet scene for half the price.

Times and Habits

If you've been out late, don't worry about missing breakfast. You can get all kinds of eggs, waffles, or pancakes at any time of day. Lunch is usually served between 11:00 A.M. and 2:30 P.M. Dinner can be as early as 5:30 P.M., but more fashionably after 7:00 P.M. Restaurants generally serve until 10:00 or 11:00 P.M.

Americans often drink coffee before, during, after, and between meals. At breakfast, and most other times, too, you may find a cup of hot coffee at your right hand as soon as you sit down. This is a gesture of hospitality. This way of providing non-stop coffee is known as "bottomless," which means that it is refilled as often as necessary without extra charge.

On American menus the "Entrées" are the main courses. Starters are listed under "Appetizers." What is called "French dressing" for salads will come as a surprise to visitors from France, who might prefer to mix their own vinaigrette. All over the United States, fish is generally served filleted, or in any case minus its head and tail—apparently for esthetic reasons.

Tipping is straightforward: 15 percent of the total on the bill (before the taxes have been added); in a case of exceptional service, go to 20 percent (see also page 125). In some restaurants you pay the cashier on the way out, after leaving a tip on the table.

Enjoy a jazz brunch in one of the many cafés in the French Quarter.

La Madeline has an impressive selection of quiche and baked goods. They also serve breakfast, lunch, and dinner.

Specialities

The Creole and Cajun vocabulary of New Orleans cuisine is usually in French, ranging in its delights from *andouilles* (spicy pork sausages) to zesty seafood sauces. However, traditions of the American south and Caribbean influences have also added certain evocative words to the menu. Some local specialities:

Beans and Rice

As in Cuba or Puerto Rico, this is a staple of local life. Red beans are cooked at length with sausage and spices, then served with boiled rice.

Oysters

Available raw—sometimes accompanied by a disclaimer about the possible dangers to life and health of *Vibrio vulnificus* bacteria—and in luscious cooked varieties such as oysters Bienville (in a cream sauce with shrimp, mushrooms, and shallots), oysters *en brochette* (skewered with bacon), oysters Rockefeller (baked with spinach or anise-soaked green vegetables), and even oyster pie.

No-nonsense diners are the perfect place to sample local fare like gumbo and po-boys.

Po-boy

The name, from "poor-boy," or, some say, the French *pourboire* (meaning "tip"), is an odd one for a sandwich any millionaire would relish. French bread is filled with combinations involving fried shrimp, oysters, soft-shell crab, roast beef, or sausage (or alligator if you choose) as well as lettuce, tomato, mayonnaise, and mustard.

A wide variety of more typical American **sandwiches** are also available in New Orleans—fat "club" sandwiches, pastrami on rye, grilled cheese sandwiches, and the "BLT" (bacon, lettuce, and tomato with mayonnaise on toast).

As with the rest of the menu, desserts in New Orleans comprise a culinary world unto themselves.

Desserts

Try fruit pies, such as apple, peach, plum, or lemon—and the regional treat, **pecan pie**. Strawberry shortcake, with biscuit topped with whipped cream, is another favourite. But to narrow it down to a single New Orleans speciality, look out for **bread pudding**, a deceptively plain name for what happens when day-old bread goes to heaven; among the secret ingredients are custard, cinnamon, nutmeg, whiskey, and raisins.

When the climate's on the muggy side, you'll probably be attracted to ice cream and frozen yoghurt, a delicious alternative to ice cream which comes in the most inventive flavours. Or try the long-lasting and portable refresher that fends off dehydration, the New Orleans **sno-ball**, consisting of crushed ice impregnated with flavoured syrup—anything from banana to watermelon.

Drinks

The local **coffee**, flavoured with roasted chicory, is so robust that it's often listed as one of the primary advantages of living in New Orleans. It can be drunk as *café au lait* (half coffee and half hot milk) or after dinner as a spectacular *café brûlot* (a flaming concoction of coffee, spices, and liqueur).

Wines from France, Italy, and California are served in many restaurants. **Beers**—imported, domestic, or the local Dixie and Abita brand—are always served ice-cold. A non-alcoholic alternative, **iced tea** is a popular accompaniment to a meal, and it's usually topped up without you having to ask, like coffee (see page 96).

A great start to a day of feasting—café au lait and beignets provide the dual fuels of sugar and caffeine.

At the elegant Brennans's you can experience bananas Foster as a taste sensation — and a visual spectacle!

Cocktails, having been invented in New Orleans (see page 79), are still very popular, and not just during Mardi Gras. Among the originals are the Sazerac (bourbon and bitters), the Ramos gin fizz, and the Hurricane (rum and juices). Other popular cocktails include Mint Juleps (a symbol of the South) and tropical rum-based drinks such as Daiquiris or Planter's Punch.

INDEX

HANDY TRAVEL TIPS

An A–Z Summary of Practical Information

A

ACCOMMODATION *(See also* CAMPING *on page* 108, YOUTH HOSTELS *on page* 128, *and* HOTELS & RESTAURANTS *from pages* 129)

Greater New Orleans offers more than 25,000 hotel rooms in all categories, from the most luxurious modern palaces to historic hostelries to budget inns. The international hotel chains are well represented; locally owned hotels include establishments with traditional trappings and hotels in renovated old mansions.

There are many bed-and-breakfast establishments and guesthouses with personalized charm and service at economical rates. Because of the sweltering summer weather, virtually every room in New Orleans, however humble, is air-conditioned. Visitors have a broad geographical choice — the heart of the French Quarter for fun seekers, the Central Business District for businessmen, or the Garden District for some stately detachment.

It's always wise to have advance reservations. This becomes absolutely essential during Mardi Gras and other special events, when New Orleans accommodation is stretched to its limit. Prices are likely to go up at those times, too.

Note that an 11% tax is added to the room rate in Orleans Parish (county) hotels, though not in bed-and-breakfast houses. There is also a "room night tax" from $1 to $3, depending on the size of the hotel.

AIRPORT

New Orleans International Airport, 24 km (15 miles) west of New Orleans, is well served by domestic airlines, but handles few international flights. To put you in the mood, five huge Mardi Gras faces look down on the terminal's main concourse. Facilities include a post office, bureau de change, restaurant, bars, shops — even a market where departing passengers can buy fresh seafood, spices, and sauces to carry aboard their flight. The airport is being expanded to accommodate a growing number of national and international visitors.

Arriving passengers will find a local tourist information office, manned by multilingual staff members, in the baggage-claim area.

New Orleans

Each international flight is met by a Gateway Receptionist, a bilingual college student in a navy-blue and white uniform. (Spanish and French are the most popular languages, but the receptionists can muster six languages in all.) In addition to porters, do-it-yourself baggage carts are available, but you have to pay $1; if you return the cart to one of the distribution points you get back 25 cents.

The taxi fare between the airport and the French Quarter or Central Business District is a flat $21 for up to three people plus $8 for each additional passenger. Allow half an hour for the trip. For $10 per person there is a shuttle bus linking the airport and hotels. A public bus also runs between the airport and the Central Business District.

B

BICYCLE RENTAL

New Orleans is flatter than Holland, hence it is a likely place to ride a bike for sightseeing or relaxation. City Park and Audubon Park are particularly agreeable, tree-shaded destinations. Bicycle rental shops are located in and near the French Quarter and in City Park. Bicycle tours are organized on weekends, covering the French Quarter or the Garden District; information from French Quarter Bicycles, 522 Dumaine, tel. 529-3136.

C

CAMPING

If you are travelling with your own lodging — recreational vehicles, campers, and trailers — you will often have to settle for rather distant campsites. Among the well-equipped sites closer to the city are Jude Travel Park, 7400 Chef Menteur Highway, New Orleans, tel. (toll-free) (800) 523-2196; and New Orleans, 70126; West KOA Campground, 11129 Jefferson Highway, River Ridge, 70123; tel. (504) 467-1792.

CAR RENTAL

Companies of international or local stature, at the airport and in the city, compete for business, so it's worth shopping around if you have the time and patience. For a list of the available firms, see the *Yellow Pages* telephone directory under Automobile Rental and Leasing. Prices vary widely under the laws of supply and demand. Generally, cars reserved long in advance cost less.

Automatic transmission and air-conditioning are standard. Note that rates sounding reasonable can end up much higher when "collision damage waiver" (CDW) and other extras are added. Check your travel insurance policy to see if you need the "personal/medical" extra; you may be fully covered.

You'll need a valid driving licence plus an International Driving Permit if your own licence is in a language other than English. Many agencies set a minimum age for car hire at 21, some at 25. A deposit as well as an advance payment may be required, though holders of major credit cards are normally exempt from this.

Driving in New Orleans poses no special problems except for a shortage of on-street parking spaces in the French Quarter. The tow-truck operators are notoriously eager to whisk away offenders who ignore or fail to understand the complex rules. Whether the car is your own or rented, you'll have to bail it out yourself.

CHILDREN

From tiny tots to teenagers, children find much to interest and amuse them in New Orleans: boat rides on the Mississippi and a wonderful ancient carousel in City Park; a streetcar ride and the "hands-on" Louisiana Children's Museum; puppet shows and history-packed plantation tours and the Aquarium. The tourist office in Jackson Square (see page 126) sells *New Orleans for Kids*, a guidebook for children including puzzles, games and suggestions for places to go and things to do.

Some hotels welcome children and are geared for babysitter service. If you think you'll need a babysitter, it's wise to make it known when you reserve your room.

New Orleans

CLIMATE

Sultry is often the word used to describe the weather in New Orleans, where the long summers tend to be mercilessly hot and the average annual rainfall is the highest of all the U.S. weather stations reporting.

The uncomfortably hot season lasts from May to October. To survive, you'll have to take it easy, stay on the shady side of the street, and make the most of the air-conditioning, which belts out full blast in hotels, restaurants, and stores. Rain, sometimes torrential, is likely between June and November, which is also the hurricane season; but New Orleans is so far inland that hurricanes rarely reach the city. The most pleasant time of year is usually early spring, a season of sunshine, blooming flowers, and Mardi Gras (see page 76).

For a weather forecast, call 465-9212. To help you with long-range predictions for your New Orleans visit, here are the average daily maximum and minimum temperatures by month:

	J	F	M	A	M	J	J	A	S	O	N	D
max °F	62	65	71	77	83	88	90	90	86	79	70	64
°C	17	18	22	25	28	31	32	32	30	26	21	18
min °F	47	50	55	61	68	74	76	76	73	64	55	48
°C	8	10	13	16	20	23	24	24	23	18	13	9

CLOTHING

Very casual lightweight clothing is all you need for sightseeing and most other daytime activities. You'll find only the fanciest restaurants will turn you away if you arrive for lunch dressed in shorts and T-shirt. In the evening a certain formality is evident in the more upscale places, some of which require men to wear a jacket and tie. In many restaurants, regardless of class, the air-conditioning can be powerful; you may find a sweater or jacket a useful defence.

COMPLAINTS

If you have a complaint about business practices, talk to the manager of the establishment. If this fails to resolve the problem, try the Better Business Bureau at 1539 Jackson Avenue, tel. 581-6222. Complaints about taxis should be directed to the Taxicab Bureau at City Hall, tel.

565-6272. For complaints about buses and streetcars, contact the Regional Transit Authority, 6700 Plaza Drive, tel. 248-3900.

CONSULATES

Most of the foreign countries maintaining diplomatic representatives in New Orleans are Latin American. Other consular addresses:

Britain: 321 Street Charles Avenue, tel. 524-4180.
France: 300 Poydras Street, tel. 523-5772.
Greece: World Trade Center, tel. 529-5288.
Italy: 630 Camp Street, tel. 524-2271.
Japan: Suite 2050, 639 Loyola Avenue, tel. 529-2101.
Norway: Suite 1700, 650 Poydras Street, tel. 522-3526.
Spain: Suite 2102, World Trade Center, tel. 525-4951.
Sweden: 2640 Canal Street, tel. 827-8600.
Switzerland: 1620 Eighth Street, tel. 897-6510.

CRIME

Like many large cities in the United States, New Orleans is experiencing a drop in crime. However, some districts are considered unsafe for lone tourists, even in broad daylight; the most notable stamping grounds of local muggers are Armstrong Park and some of the cemeteries. After dark it's best to shun dimly lit streets, both as a pedestrian and when it comes to finding a parking space for your car.

During Mardi Gras and other crowded occasions, pickpockets are almost certain to be in attendance. Leave valuables and reserves of cash, traveller's cheques, airline tickets, etc., in your hotel safe, and make sure your handbag is securely fastened or your wallet is in an inside pocket. Never leave belongings unattended, or visible in a car.

CUSTOMS and ENTRY REGULATIONS

For a stay of less than 90 days British visitors with a valid ten-year passport and a return ticket on a major airline do not generally need a U.S. visa. Nationals of most other European countries are given the same priority. Canadian visitors merely have to show proof of nationality. For further details consult your travel agent or a U.S.

consulate. If you do need a visa, application forms are available through travel agents, airlines, or U.S. consulates. Allow at least a month for postal applications. Forms must be accompanied by a passport valid for at least six months longer than the intended visit, a passport-size photo, evidence of possession of sufficient funds for the duration of the stay, and proof of intent to leave the United States after the visit. A health certificate is not normally required.

Red and green channels are in operation at America's international airports. If you fly in, you should be given the customs and immigration forms to complete well before landing.

The chart below shows certain duty-free items a non-resident may take into the U.S. (if you are over 21) and, when returning home, into your own country.

A non-resident may take into the United States gifts, free of duty and taxes, to the value of $100. Importing plants, seeds, vegetables, fruits, or other fresh food is prohibited; foods of all kinds are subject to inspection. If you're carrying money and cheques totalling more than $10,000 in or out of the country they must be reported.

	Cigarettes		Cigars		Tobacco	Spirits		Wine
U.S.A.	200	or	50	or	1,350 g	1 l	or	1 l
Australia	200	or	250 g	or	250 g	1 l	or	1 l
Canada	200	and	50	and	900 g	1.1 l	or	1.1 l
Eire	200	or	50	or	150 g	1 l	and	2 l
N. Zealand	200	or	50	or	250 g	1.1 l	and	4.5 l
S. Africa	400	and	50	and	250 g	1 l.	and	2 l
U.K.	200	or	50	or	250 g	1 l	and	2 l

D

DRIVING

The rule in the United States is to drive on the right and overtake on the left. In Louisiana you can turn right at a red light, unless there's a sign to the contrary, providing you stop and check that no traffic or pedestrians impede this manoeuvre. Seat belts are obligatory for the driver and front-seat passenger. Children of four years and under must also be buckled in. School buses (always painted yellow) are given the respect of royal processions in the United States. It's a serious offence to pass a school bus *in either direction* on a two-lane road when it is taking on or discharging passengers.

Speed limits. Under Louisiana law the speed limit is 105 km/h (65 mph) on an interstate highway in rural areas. On all other highways the limit is 90km/h (55mph).

Driving conditions. "Lane discipline" on highways, well developed elsewhere in the country, counts for little in relaxed New Orleans, where drivers cut in and out of lanes on a whim, often without signalling. Be wary at stop lights, where the yellow may inspire haste instead of caution. Many street signs in New Orleans are hard to find until you're accustomed to the system; some tend to be high up in the centre of divided streets. No-parking signs are deceptive. On the highway, exit signs are clear, but other details may be left to your intuition. Drive carefully in the bayou country, where you might have to swerve to avoid a turtle crossing the road . . . or an alligator.

Petrol/gas stations. Some stations close early and on Sundays. Most are self-service; "full-serve" (which may include a window clean) is more expensive.

Parking. New Orleans is a very friendly city, except when it comes to parking cars. Towaways are legion. The Department of Streets, Parking Division, issues a booklet, *Park Smart in New Orleans*, explaining some of the complexities of the local regulations. For instance, you could be towed away for parking within 6 metres (about 20 feet) of any street corner or crosswalk or traffic signal or within 4.5 metres (15 feet) of a fire hydrant. If your car has disap-

Fluid measures

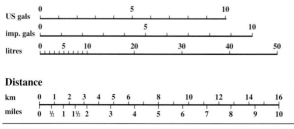

Distance

peared, phone the Claiborne Auto Pound, tel. 565-7450, to ascertain whether it is in their custody. For the convenience of its many anxious customers, the pound, at 400 N. Claiborne Avenue, is open from 7:30am to 10:30pm daily. To bail out your car will cost $75 for the towing "service" plus a fine. Visa and MasterCard are welcome.

E

ELECTRIC CURRENT

Throughout the United States the standard is 110 volts, 60 cycle AC. Plugs usually have two flat prongs. Overseas visitors without dual-voltage travel appliances will need a transformer and adapter plug for appliances such as an electric razor or hair dryer.

EMERGENCIES (*See* HEALTH AND MEDICAL CARE *on page* 116 *and* POLICE *on page* 122)

The all-purpose emergency number is **911**. Dial **0** for the operator.

ETIQUETTE

You'll have to get used to American informality; don't be startled if the hotel desk clerk calls you by your first name, or if a new acquaintance starts asking intimate questions. Handshakes are prevalent but exchanging business cards is not an automatic part of introductions. Certain elements of politeness are pronounced, such as the American use of "Sir" or "Ma'am," even when summoning a waiter or waitress. "Thank you" is answered by "you're welcome" or "you're quite welcome," "quite" meaning "very."

G

GETTING TO NEW ORLEANS

Because of the complexity and variability of the fare structure, you need the advice of an informed, trustworthy travel agent well before you propose to visit New Orleans.

By Air

International flights. Relatively few flights from overseas go to New Orleans, and most of those originate in Latin America. But New Orleans International Airport averages about 150 domestic flights a day, permitting various connections from gateway cities.

Beyond the first-class, business/club, and economy fares, the principal cost-cutting possibilities are variations of APEX. Certain U.S. airlines also offer bargains for foreign travellers who visit several American destinations.

Domestic flights. Among the airlines serving New Orleans are American, Continental, Delta, Northwest, TWA, United, and USAir. There are non-stop or one-stop flights to many U.S. cities.

Baggage. Scheduled transatlantic flights allow you to check in two pieces of baggage of normal size. The same applies on flights within North America. On other international flights the allowance varies between 20 kg (44 pounds) and 40 kg (88 pounds) depending on the class in which you are travelling. In addition to checked baggage, one piece of hand luggage which fits under the aircraft seat may be carried on board. It is advisable to insure all your luggage for the duration of your trip, possibly as part of a travel insurance package.

By Rail

Amtrak, the American passenger railway company, runs daily trains between New Orleans, New York, and Chicago. The three-times-a-week train from Los Angeles to New Orleans takes 45 hours and continus on to Miami, Florida. Special package tours are available. Permanent residents of countries outside the United States and Canada are eligible to buy USA Rail Passes covering 45 days of unlimited travel on Amtrak. If your travel agent can't help, write to Amtrak International Sales, 60 Massachusetts Avenue N.E., Washington, DC 20002. In the United States, tel. 1-800-USA-RAIL.

By Bus

Greyhound buses share the air-conditioned Union Passenger Terminal (at 1001 Loyola Avenue) with Amtrak. There are "rover passes" for specified periods of unlimited travel, but some of these can only be bought outside the United States. For information about bus services across the continent, call Greyhound on 1-800-231-2222.

By Car

The interstate highway linking Florida and California, the I-10, passes through — in fact, over — New Orleans. Its route had been set to penetrate the most historic part of the city before civic action diverted it. The French Quarter is only a few blocks from the I-10 via the Vieux Carré exit. For the CBD use the Poydras Street exit.

GUIDES and TOURS

With tourism one of the city's four biggest industries (the others are oil, gas, and the port), New Orleans is well organized for all kinds of guided tours. There are brief orientation tours, all-day sightseeing rounds, combination bus-and-boat tours, walking tours, nightlife tours, and special-interest tours. Farther afield, you can take a tour of plantations or the bayou, or a long or short excursion on a Mississippi paddlewheeler.

Hotel lobbies and the tourist office (see page 126) are well supplied with leaflets outlining the alternative offers. Most tour companies are geared to provide guides who speak foreign languages, but some advance notice may be required.

H

HEALTH and MEDICAL CARE

New Orleans is well equipped with medical facilities meeting the highest standards, most notably the Tulane University Medical Center, 1415 Tulane Avenue. As everywhere in the United States, though, health care is extremely expensive, so it's essential that you sign up for medical insurance covering your stay before you leave home. This can be arranged through an insurance company or agent or through your travel agent as part of a travel insurance package.

Standards of hygiene are high and the tap water is drinkable. The only health hazard you are likely to encounter is the sun; in summer it's wise to wear a hat, apply sunscreen, and stay in the shade. You might also need insect repellent during the mosquito season.

Drugstores *(pharmacies).* On the edge of the French Quarter, the Walgreens drugstore at 900 Canal St., is open until 9pm. Farther out, two drugstores are open 24 hours: Walgreens at 3311 Canal Street and K&B at 7060 Veterans Boulevard, Metairie. You may find that some medicines obtainable over the counter in your home country are available only on prescription in the United States, and vice versa.

L

LANGUAGE

Even Americans may have some problems in New Orleans, home of rich accents and dialect. The French background accounts for some of the eccentricities: the word for sidewalk (British "pavement") is *banquette,* mispronounced with the accent on the first syllable, and many local gastronomical terms, from *andouille* (a sausage) to *pain perdu* (French toast), reflect the city's French history. You'll find, however, that the overwhelming majority of the people of New Orleans speak little or no French.

To help with a few of the most common Anglo-American linguistic misunderstandings, here's a brief glossary:

U.S.	British
bill	banknote
check	bill (restaurant)
collect call	reverse-charge call
dead end	cul-de-sac
elevator	lift
faucet	tap
first floor	ground floor
gas(oline)	petrol
kerosene	paraffin
liquor	spirits
U.S.	British
pants	trousers
purse/pocketbook	handbag

second floor	first floor
subway	underground
suspenders	braces
underpass	subway
undershirt	vest
vest	waistcoat

LAUNDRY and DRY-CLEANING

Express laundry and dry-cleaning services are available in most hotels. If money is a factor you can seek out a neighbourhood laundry or cleaning establishment; same-day or even 1-hour service may be offered. Launderettes (laundromats), self-service with coin-operated washing machines and dryers, are a cheaper alternative.

LIQUOR REGULATIONS

Most American cities have restrictions on drinking, but in New Orleans the bars are permitted to operate 24 hours a day. Grocery stores and other outlets dispense bottles round the clock. Drinking on the street from a bottle, glass, or can is illegal, so plastic cups, usually equipped with straws, are much in evidence. The legal age for drinking in New Orleans is 21. You might be asked to prove your age by showing some identification ("ID").

LOST PROPERTY

If you lose your passport, get in touch with your consulate immediately (see page 126). If you leave anything on a bus or streetcar, it may turn up at the lost-and-found department of the Regional Transit Authority, 6700 Plaza Drive, tel. 242-2600. Or try the police department, tel. 821-2222.

MAPS

Useful maps for walking and driving tours are available free of charge from the Greater New Orleans Tourist and Convention Bureau (see page 126). News-stands and bookstores also sell maps of the city and state. Maps of Louisiana and nearby states are sold at many petrol (gas) stations.

MONEY MATTERS

Currency. The dollar ($) is divided into 100 cents (¢).

Banknotes: $1, $2 (rare), $5, $10, $20, $50, and $100. Larger denominations are not in general circulation. All notes are the same size and same black-and-green colour (except for the anomalous new $50 and $100 bills), so double-check your cash before you dispense it.

Coins: 1¢ (known as a penny), 5¢ (nickel), 10¢ (dime), 25¢ (quarter), 50¢ (half dollar), and $1. The dollar coin is relatively rare and can be difficult to negotiate, though the U.S. Post Office often (and inconveniently) dispenses $1 coins as change.

Banks and currency exchange. Banks are open from 9am to 3 or 4pm Monday to Friday. You can change foreign currency at the airport, at banks, and at bureaux de change such as Thomas Cook Currency Service, 111 St. Charles Avenue; or American Express Travel Agency, 158 Baronne Street.

Credit cards. When buying something or paying a restaurant bill you may be asked "Cash or charge?" In the United States "plastic money" is a way of life. Most Americans carry a variety of credit cards, and they are accepted in most places. But you may be asked for supplementary identification.

Traveller's cheques. Banks, stores, restaurants, and hotels almost universally accept dollar-denominated traveller's cheques as the equivalent of cash. It's straightforward if the cheques are issued by American Express or an American bank, much less so if the issuer is not well known in the U.S. If your traveller's cheques are in foreign denominations, they can be changed only in a few banks with experience in international transactions. Exchange only small amounts at a time, keeping the balance in your hotel safe if possible. Keep a record of the serial numbers in a separate place to facilitate a refund in the event of loss or theft.

New Orleans

Sales taxes. The price tag only tells part of the story. Louisiana sales tax and New Orleans city tax are added at the cash register. Shoppers from abroad can recover these amounts on certain purchases from participating retailers under a pioneering scheme called Louisiana Tax Free Shopping (LTFS) (see SHOPPING, page 84). Not all stores collaborate with this project, and some paperwork is involved, but you can get a tax refund at the airport. Ask the tourist office (see page 126) for an 80-page brochure on duty-free shopping, containing all the details you'll need.

PLANNING YOUR BUDGET

To give you an idea of what to expect, here are some average prices of interest to visitors. They can only be approximate, as inflation takes its toll, and because prices vary greatly between one establishment or neighbourhood and another.

Airport transfer. Taxi to French Quarter or Central Business District $21 for up to three passengers; $8 each additional passenger. Shuttle bus $10 per person.

Babysitters. $7 per hour ($1 per additional child) plus $10 taxi fare.

Bicycle rental. $4-5 per hour, $12-16.50 per day.

Buses and streetcars. $1.10 for standard transport, $1.25 express, $1.25 Riverfront streetcar. Transfers 10¢. $4 for 2-day pass, $8 for 3-day pass.

Car rental. Depending on the company, the season, even the time of day you inquire, prices can range from $15 to $50 per day; cheaper by the week.

Car park (parking lots). $2 per hour, $3.50 and up per day. (Covered garages cost more.)

Camping. $16-26 with full hookup.

Cleaning, laundry. Suit $6, shirt $1.50.

Entertainment. Cinema $6, concert $10-60, disco/nightclub/jazz club cover charge up to $20 or minimum 2 drinks.

Hairdressers. Woman's cut $15 and up, man's cut $10.

Hotels (double occupancy, per night: 11% tax is added). Expensive: $125 and up, moderate $75-100, budget $50-75 (see pages 130-136).

Meals and drinks (tax is added). Breakfast $3-10, lunch $5-15, dinner $15 and up, beer $2-4, spirit $3-6, soft drink $1, coffee $1.

Shoeshine. $3.

Taxis. $2.10 when meter starts plus $1 per mile or 30¢ per minute; 75¢ for each additional passenger.

Tours. Half-day city tour $16, combined bus/boat tour $26, full-day plantation tour $33, swamp tour $35.

N

NEWSPAPERS and MAGAZINES

Once a highly competitive newspaper town, New Orleans now supports only one daily newspaper, the *Times-Picayune.* It lists the major events, most comprehensively on Fridays in its entertainment supplement, titled *Lagniappe.* Another regular good listings source is a weekly giveaway called *Gambit.* Hotels distribute free tourist magazines like *This Week in New Orleans* and *Where. New Orleans* magazine, a monthly, lists events and covers general and cultural news. *Offbeat* magazine, also a monthly, provides the best music coverage of the city.

Nationally distributed newspapers — *The New York Times,* the *Wall Street Journal,* and *USA Today* — are available from vending machines. Newspapers and magazines from Britain, France, Germany, Italy, and beyond may be found at Lenny's News, 622 S. Carrollton, just off St. Charles Avenue. Another source of foreign publications is Sidney's, 917 Decatur Street, in the French Quarter.

O

OPENING HOURS

Department stores in the Central Business District are open Monday to Saturday from 9:45 or 10am to 5:30 or 6pm; shopping malls, however, stay open later. In the French Quarter, shops catering to tourists may remain open late into the evening and on Sunday.

New Orleans

(Drinking establishments in the French Quarter may keep going 24 hours a day.)

Museum hours vary but they tend to be open between 10am and 4 or 5pm. Most are closed on Mondays, some on Tuesdays as well. Out of town, **plantations** are open daily except on major holidays.

Banks are open between 9am and 3 or 4pm Monday to Friday.

The French Quarter branch of the **post office** operates from 8:30am to 4:30pm Monday to Friday, and the main post office, at 701 Loyola Ave., opens on Saturday mornings as well.

P

PHOTOGRAPHY and VIDEO

All the well-known brands of film and equipment are sold in New Orleans. Same-day or one-hour processing is available for colour prints; transparencies (colour slides) take longer.

X-ray machines operated by airport security personnel do not harm ordinary film, but if you're using very high-speed film you can ask for hand inspection. A bigger threat to your film is the summer heat of New Orleans. Never leave your camera or film rolls in a car parked in the sun.

Blank video tape is available for all types of camera. (But note that pre-recorded tapes made for the U.S. market won't work on European systems, and conversion is expensive.)

POLICE

The blue-uniformed city police are deployed on foot, on motorbikes, on horseback, and mostly in patrol cars. They courteously assist the tourists, who contribute $2.6 billion per year to the local economy. In an emergency dial **911**. (In a non-emergency, dial 821-2222.)

POST OFFICES

The U.S. Postal Service deals only with mail. The main post office, in the CBD at 701 Loyola Avenue, is open from 9am to 4:30pm Monday to Friday and Saturday from 8am to 1pm. Branches —

including the French Quarter post office at 1022 Iberville Street — are closed Saturday.

Commercial mailing firms sell stamps and wrap packages, adding a service charge. Vending machines selling stamps, at marked-up prices, may be found in drugstores, souvenir shops, and transport terminals. U.S. mail boxes are blue and usually located at street corners.

Poste restante (general delivery). If you don't know where you'll be staying and you want to receive mail, have it sent to you care of General Delivery, 701 Loyola Avenue, New Orleans, LA 70140. You can pick it up at the main post office, where general delivery mail is held for 30 days. You'll have to show identification. American Express also holds mail for foreign visitors (without charge if you have their credit card or traveller's cheques).

PUBLIC HOLIDAYS

When certain holidays (such as Christmas) fall on a Sunday, banks, post offices, and most stores close on the following Monday. They close on Friday if those holidays fall on a Saturday. In addition to the customary American occasions, New Orleans observes two holidays little noted in the rest of the United States: All Saints' Day and Mardi Gras.

January 1	*New Year's Day*
July 4	*Independence Day*
November 1	*All Saints' Day*
November 11	*Veterans' Day*
December 25	*Christmas Day*

Moveable dates

January	*Martin Luther King Jr Day*
February	*President's Day*
February or March	*Mardi Gras*
May	*Memorial Day*
September	*Labor Day*
October	*Columbus Day*
November	*Thanksgiving*
November	*Election Day*

R

RADIO and TV

The local television network stations are WWL (CBS, Channel 4), WDSU (NBC, Channel 6), and WVUE (ABC, Channel 8). Programmes of the Public Broadcasting Service (PBS), usually less trivial than the commercial networks, are on Channel 12. Many hotels also offer CNN, the 24-hour news channel.

There are many radio stations to choose from on AM and FM. WWOZ, 90.7FM, plays all varieties of local music. WWNO, 89.9FM, "Classical New Orleans," is commercial-free. In Cajun country you'll pick up bilingual (French/English) stations playing Louisiana country music.

RELIGIOUS SERVICES

New Orleans is a predominantly Roman-Catholic city but there are Protestant churches — Baptist, Episcopal, Lutheran, Methodist, Presbyterian, and others. Hotel concierges have lists of addresses and times of services.

S

SMOKING

As in most of the United States, smoking is prohibited in many public places such as schools, libraries, theatre lobbies, public restrooms, and service or check-out lines. Restaurants that seat more than 50 customers are required to reserve a large no-smoking section. Domestic airlines prohibit smoking on board, even on long flights.

T

TELEPHONES

The American telephone system is run by private, regional companies. Coin- or card-operated phones are found in all public places — hotel lobbies, drugstores, filling stations, bars, restaurants, and along the streets. Directions for use are clearly stated on the machine. For local directory assistance dial 1-411.

When calling long distance, the rules of competition mean that you often have to choose between companies by pushing one or another button; but to the visitor it scarcely matters which. Evening (after 5pm) and weekend rates are much cheaper. Many hotels, airlines and business firms have toll-free numbers (beginning 1-800-) so you can avoid long-distance charges.

Some hotels add a hefty surcharge on outgoing calls, local or long-distance. If it seems exorbitant you can go out to use a pay phone, but you'll have to have a hoard of coins at the ready and an electronic voice may break in to tell you to insert more. Credit cards may now also be used for telephone calls.

Faxes and telegrams. The telegraph companies (you'll find them in the *Yellow Pages*) are privately run. Offering domestic and overseas telex and telegraph services, they specialize in electronic transfers of money. For quick written communication, the most practical means is sending a fax. Facsimile service is available in hotels (the business service bureau or the desk) as well as in commercial locations such as stationery stores, copying firms, and even drugstores.

TIME DIFFERENCES

New Orleans is in the U.S. Central time zone, which is 6 hours behind GMT. Between the first Sunday in April and the last Sunday in October, the clock is advanced 1 hour for Daylight Saving Time (GMT minus 5 hours). These dates are not quite synchronized with the changes in other countries. The following shows the time in other cities in summer when it is noon in New Orleans.

Los Angeles	**New Orleans**	New York	London	Paris
10am	**noon**	1pm	6pm	7pm

Note also that Americans customarily write dates in a different order from the day/month/year system of Europe. Thus 1/6/99 in the United States means 6 January 1999.

New Orleans

TIPPING

You are expected to add about 15% to restaurant *and* bar bills — based on the total of the bill excluding tax. If service has been exceptionally good, 20% is appropriate. Cinema or theatre ushers are not tipped, but doormen, cloakroom attendants, etc. should be remunerated — no less than 50 cents. Some general guidelines:

Porter	50¢-$1 per bag (minimum $1)
Hotel maid	$1 per day
	(except for very short stays)
Lavatory attendant	50¢
Taxi driver	about 15%
Tour guide	10-15%
Hairdresser/barber	15%

TOILETS

You can use a wide range of expressions to avoid, at all costs, calling a toilet a toilet: "restroom," "powder room," "bathroom," "comfort station," "ladies' room," "men's room," — the list is endless. Public lavatories are few, but in town you'll usually find facilities in a bar, restaurant, big hotel, or department store.

TOURIST INFORMATION

For advance inquiries, write to the Greater New Orleans Tourist and Convention Commission, Inc., 1520 Sugar Bowl Drive, New Orleans, LA 70112, tel. (504) 566-5011 or (800) 672-6124. The Commission's offices are well stocked with free maps and brochures at the airport and in the French Quarter, facing Jackson Square, at 529 St. Ann Street. For an introduction to the "Soul of New Orleans" contact the Greater New Orleans Black Tourism Network at 523-5652. Information about trips farther afield is available at the same St. Ann Street location, an office of the Louisiana State Department of Culture, Recreation and Tourism (tel. 568-5661).

TRANSPORT

The buses and streetcars of New Orleans are operated by the Regional Transport Authority (RTA). The most useful lines for tourists are the Riverfront streetcar, the historic St. Charles streetcar line, and the small Vieux Carré bus (designed to resemble an old streetcar) making a circuit through the French Quarter and downtown. You must deposit the exact fare in the coin-and-banknote collecting machine alongside the driver, who carries no change. VisiTour Passes cover unlimited travel on all streetcar and bus lines — $4 for one day and $8 for three days. They are sold at some hotels and stores.

For a colourful voyage, a **ferry** carries cars and passengers between Canal Street and the Algiers district. Passengers ride free. Note that the last ferry of the day leaves for Algiers at 9:30pm and doesn't return until the next morning.

Taxis are plentiful, especially where tourists congregate. You can hail one in the street or go to any of the big hotels, where they tend to lie in wait. Cabs are metered; extras are listed on a sign in the passenger compartment. A 15% tip is customary.

TRAVELLERS WITH DISABILITIES

The United States is a leader in catering to people with special needs — for example, public buildings re required by law to have ramps and toilets designed for wheelchair-bound travellers, and Braille numbers alongside floor buttons in lifts. In *New Orleans Lodging*, issued by the New Orleans Tourist & Convention Commission (see page 126), many of the entries include information on access for those with mobility difficulties. For more information contact the Advocacy Center for the Elderly and Disabled at 522-2337.

W

WATER

New Orleans water, much purified from the generous and conveniently located Mississippi River, is safe to drink. You'll also find bottled waters, local and imported.

New Orleans

WEIGHTS and MEASURES

(For fluid and distance measures see DRIVING on page 111.) Efforts to ease the United States into the metric system are proceeding centimetre by centimetre. The government itself is said to be converting to international measurements, but in real life it's still inches, feet, yards, miles, and degrees Fahrenheit.

Length

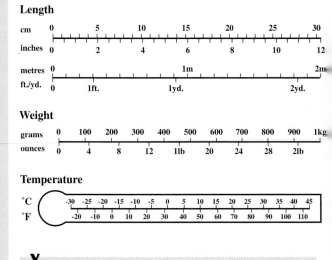

Weight

Temperature

Y

YOUTH HOSTELS

In an appealing location in the Garden District, an international youth hostel occupies an antebellum mansion, Marquette House, at 2253 Carondelet Street, tel. 523-3014. There is also a modern YMCA Center with accommodation for men and women at Lee Circle, 920 St. Charles Avenue, tel. 568-9622.

Recommended Hotels

To help you choose a hotel, the following list is a selection based on the criteria of price, quality, and location. The hotels are listed in alphabetical order. The following symbols apply for a single room:

✪	less than $50
✪✪	$50-$75
✪✪✪	$75-$100
✪✪✪✪	$100-$125
✪✪✪✪✪	$125-$250 upwards

Note that prices are generally higher during Mardi Gras and other special occasions.

Bienville House Hotel ✪✪✪ *320 Decatur Street, New Orleans 70130; tel. (504) 529-2345, toll-free (800) 535-7836.* Between Bourbon Street and the Aquarium of the Americas, 81 individually decorated rooms, two suites, courtyard, pool.

Bourbon Orleans Hotel ✪✪✪ – ✪✪✪✪ *717 Orleans Street, New Orleans 70112; tel. (504) 523-2222, toll-free (800) 521-5338; fax (504) 525-8166.* Restored landmark in the heart of the French Quarter at Bourbon Street. Canopied beds, Chippendale and magnificent Queen Anne furniture, and marble bathrooms. 164 rooms plus 47 bi-level suites.

Château Hotel ✪✪ *1001 Rue Chartres, New Orleans 70116; tel. (504) 524-9636; fax (504) 525-2989.* 45 recently refurbished rooms surrounding an 18th-century patio. Free parking.

Chateau Le Moyne Holiday Inn ✪✪✪–✪✪✪✪ *301 Dauphine Street, New Orleans 70112; tel. (504) 581-1303, toll-*

free (800) HOLIDAY. The most charming of several Holiday Inns around town, incorporating four Greek-Revival townhouses. 159 rooms, 12 suites.

Cornstalk Hotel ✿✿✿ *915 Royal Street, New Orleans 70140; tel. (504) 523-1515.* Chandeliers and four-poster beds are among the many charms of this hotel — a French Quarter landmark because of its ornate cast-iron "cornstalk fence" (see page 45).

Doubletree Hotel ✿✿✿✿ *300 Canal Street, New Orleans 70130; tel. (504) 599-3023, toll-free (800) 222-TREE; fax (504) 599-3000.* Just opposite the French Quarter near the riverfront, 363 modern rooms plus 15 suites. Good facilities include a swimming pool and health club.

Fairmont Hotel ✿✿✿ *123 Baronne Street, New Orleans 70140; tel. (504) 529-7111, toll-free (800) 527-4727; fax. (504) 522-2203.* Rich in history, this hangout of Huey Long's is just beyond the French Quarter. Proclaimed as "The Grande Dame of hotels in the Deep South," it has 12 floors and 615 rooms, plus 85 suites. Heated pool and floodlit tennis courts.

Grenoble House ✿✿✿✿ *329 Dauphine Street, New Orleans 70122; tel. (504) 522-1331, toll-free (800) 722-1834; fax (504) 224-4968.* A restored 19th-century complex offering tranquillity in the heart of the French Quarter. 17 uniquely furnished suites. Pool, jacuzzi.

Holiday Inn French Quarter ✿✿✿✿ *124 Royal Street at Iberville, New Orleans 70130; tel. (504) 529-7211, toll-free (800) 747-3279; fax (504) 566-1127.* Surprisingly set above a 9-storey parking garage. 252 rooms, 56 suites. Indoor pool.

Hotel de la Poste ✪✪✪ – ✪✪✪✪ *316 Chartres Street, New Orleans 70130; tel. (504) 581-1200, toll-free (800) 448-4927; fax (504) 523-2910.* 87 rooms plus 13 suites, newly renovated in the heart of the French Quarter. Patio, pool.

Hotel Inter-Continental New Orleans ✪✪✪✪✪ *444 St. Charles Avenue, New Orleans; tel. (504) 525-5566; fax. (504) 585-4387.* In the financial district, near the French Quarter, 462 luxurious rooms plus 20 suites; restaurants, pool, and business center.

Hotel Maison de Ville ✪✪✪✪✪ *727 Toulouse Street, New Orleans 70130; tel. (504) 561-5858, toll-free (800) 634-1600; fax (504) 528-9739.* Luxurious French Quarter hideaway with 16 rooms, 7 cottages.

Hotel St. Pierre ✪✪✪ *911 Burgundy Street, New Orleans 70116; tel. (504) 524-4401 toll-free (800)225-4040; fax (504) 524-6800.* In 18th-century French Quarter cottages, 66 rooms, nine suites, two pools.

Hotel Villa Convento ✪✪ *616 Ursulines Street, New Orleans 70116; tel. (504) 522-1793; fax (504) 524-1902.* Family-run 19th-century townhouse in the French Quarter. 25 rooms.

Lamothe House ✪✪ – ✪✪✪✪ *621 Esplanade Avenue, New Orleans 70116; tel. (504) 947-1161, toll-free (800) 367-5858; fax (504) 943-6536.* On the edge of the French Quarter, this charming hotel offers 11 rooms plus 9 suites in a stately historic atmosphere of a columned mansion and former slave quarters. Antique furnishings complement modern bathrooms.

Le Meridien New Orleans ✪✪✪✪✪ *614 Canal Street, New Orleans; tel. (504) 525-6500, toll-free (800) 543-4300; fax*

New Orleans

(504) 586-1543. Just across Canal Street from the French Quarter, a modern French-owned luxury hotel with 494 luxury rooms including seven suites; French-speaking concierge.

Le Pavillon Hotel ✪✪✪ *833 Poydras Street, New Orleans; tel. (504) 581-3111, toll-free (800) 535-9095; fax (504) 522-5433.* An astonishing windowless Neo-classical façade — complete with top-hatted doorman, both winter and summer — announce this European-style hotel in the Central Business District. Founded in 1907, it has 220 rooms and a rooftop pool.

Le Richelieu ✪✪✪ *1234 Chartres Street, New Orleans 70116; tel. (504) 529-2492, toll-free (800) 535-9653; fax (504) 524-8179.* Friendly motor hotel situated in the French Quarter. 69 rooms and 17 suites plus free parking on the premises. Swimming pool, tropical patio.

Marriott Hotel ✪✪✪✪✪ *555 Canal Street, New Orleans 70140; tel. (504) 581-1000, toll-free (800) 228-9290; fax. (504) 581-5749.* Giant convention-style skyscraper hotel on the edge of the French Quarter. You could get lost among the 1,236 rooms and 54 suites.

Monteleone Hotel ✪✪✪✪ *214 Royal Street, New Orleans 70140; tel. (504) 523-3341, toll-free (800) 535-9595; fax (504) 528-1019.* A century-old tradition, chandeliers and all, in the French Quarter's finest shopping street. 600 rooms, 35 suites, restaurants, pool.

New Orleans Hilton Riverside and Towers ✪✪✪✪✪ *Poydras at the Mississippi River, New Orleans 70140; tel. (504) 561-0500, toll-free (800) 445-8667; fax (504) 568-1721.* A huge but enviably sited hotel complex along the river: 1,602 rooms plus 82 suites. Wide range of facilities from outdoor pools and indoor and outdoor tennis courts to five restaurants and Pete Fountain's jazz.

Nottoway Plantation ✪✪✪✪ - ✪✪✪✪✪ *Mississippi River Road, 30765, White Castle LA 70788; tel. (504) 545-2730; fax (504) 545-2730.* 10 rooms plus 3 suites in the vast mansion, or the Overseer's cottage. Restaurant.

Oak Alley Plantation ✪✪✪ *6745 Louisiana Highway 18, Vacherie, LA 70090; tel. (504) 265-2151.* Five beautiful renovated 19th-century cottages situated right on the wonderfully photogenic plantation grounds (see page 65). Restaurant.

Olivier House Hotel ✪✪✪ *828 Toulouse Street, New Orleans 70112; tel. (504) 525-8456; fax (504) 529-2006.* Quirky, historic and family-run French Quarter guesthouse, with 28 rooms and 12 suites, each uniquely furnished. There's also a parrot in the jungly patio.

Omni Royal Orleans Hotel ✪✪✪✪✪ *621 St. Louis Street, New Orleans 70140; tel. (504) 529-5333, toll-free (800) THE-OMNI; fax (504) 529-7016.* Lavish, elegant marble recreation of 19th-century French Quarter luxury. 326 rooms plus 25 suites. Marble baths, rooftop pool, gym.

Place d'Armes Hotel ✪✪✪ *625 St. Ann Street, New Orleans 70116; tel. (504) 524-4531 toll-free (800) 366-2743; fax (504) 581-3802.* The only hotel on Jackson Square, the heart of the French Quarter, a restored 18th-century complex of 74 rooms, 8 suites; pool and patio.

Pontchartrain Hotel ✪✪✪✪✪ *2031 St. Charles Street, New Orleans 70140; tel. (504) 524-0581, toll-free (800) 777-6193;*

fax (504) 524-7828. Old favourite remembered for personalized service. A celebrity hideout on the St. Charles streetcar line in the Garden District. 61 guest rooms and 40 suites.

Prytania Park Hotel ✪✪✪ *1525 Prytania Street, New Orleans 70130; tel. (504) 524-0427 toll-free (800) 862-1984; fax (504) 522-2977.* In the Garden District, a few steps from the streetcar line, is this complex of 56 rooms and 6 suites, most of them modern, but some 19th-century traditional.

Quality Inn Maison St. Charles ✪✪✪ *1319 St. Charles Avenue, New Orleans; tel. (504) 522-0187, toll-free (800) 831-1783; fax (504) 525-2218.* 132 rooms and 20 suites in a complex of five restored antebellum homes in the Garden District.

Radisson Hotel New Orleans ✪✪✪✪ *1500 Canal Street, New Orleans 70130; tel. (504) 522-4500, toll-free (800) 843-4833.* 18-storey hotel in the Central Business District, 759 rooms, rooftop pool, gym.

Royal Sonesta Hotel ✪✪✪✪–✪✪✪✪✪ *300 Bourbon Street, New Orleans 70140; tel. (504) 586-0300, toll-free (800) 766-3782; fax (504) 586-0335.* 500-room landmark at the centre of the French Quarter. Various styles, sizes, and prices of rooms.

Sheraton New Orleans ✪✪✪✪✪ *500 Canal Street, New Orleans 70130; tel. (504) 525-2500, toll-free (800) 253-6156; fax (504) 592-5615.* 1,100 rooms and 72 suites for businessmen and conventioneers, across Canal Street from the French Quarter. Striking lobby. Multiple restaurants, bars, cafés, health club, and all services.

Soniat House ✪✪✪✪ *1133 Chartres Street, New Orleans, tel. (504) 522-0570, toll-free (800) 544-8808; fax (504) 522-7208.* A historic architectural gem in the French Quarter converted into a luxurious, intimate hotel with 19 rooms and 12 suites, furnished with antiques.

St. Charles Inn ✪✪ *3636 St. Charles Avenue, New Orleans; tel. (504) 899-8888.* Uptown, 40 comfortable rooms on the St. Charles Avenue streetcar line.

St. Charles Guest House ✪ *1748 Prytania Street, New Orleans 70130; tel. (504) 523-6556; fax (504) 522-6340.* 23 economical rooms, 1 suite, and a pool to be found in this cozy bed-and-breakfast establishment in the Lower Garden District.

St. Peter House ✪ – ✪✪ *1005 St. Peter Street, New Orleans 70116; tel. (504) 524-9232; toll-free (800) 535-7815; fax (504) 523-5198.* 19th-century atmosphere in the French Quarter with 17 rooms and 6 suites.

Westin Canal Place ✪✪✪✪✪ *100 Rue Iberville, New Orleans 70130; tel. (504) 566-7006, toll-free (800) 228-3000; fax 553-5133.* Built above the Canal Place shopping mall. All 397 rooms and 38 suites have excellent views of the river and the city; rooftop pool.

Windsor Court Hotel ✪✪✪✪✪ *300 Gravier Street, New Orleans 70130; tel. (504) 523-6000, toll-free (800) 262-2662; fax (504) 553-5133.* The ultimate in modern luxury near the Mississippi; a $5-million art collection decorates public and guest rooms. 23 floors, 324 rooms, of which 266 are suites. Health club, pool.

Recommended Restaurants

Here is a selection of restaurants appreciated by recent travellers. If you find other places worth recommending we'd be pleased to hear from you.

To give you an idea of the price range, the following symbols apply for a three-course meal for one, but remember that tips, taxes, and drinks will drive the bill up.

✪	below $15
✪✪	around $20
✪✪✪	$25-$35 or more

Reservations are recommended at smarter restaurants, where men may be required to wear jackets.

FRENCH QUARTER

Acme Oyster House ✪ *724 Iberville Street, New Orleans; tel. 522-5973.* Here everything revolves around the oyster bar, where faithful customers have been eating oysters on the half shell or fried since early in the 20th century. Shrimp and catfish, too. Casual atmosphere.

Alex Patout's ✪✪ *221 Royal Street, New Orleans; tel. 525-7788.* Authentic Creole cooking. Considering the fashionable surroundings and the quality of the food, good value for money. Strong on seafood. Dressy. Open for dinner only.

Antoine's ✪✪✪ *713 St. Louis Street, New Orleans; tel. 581-4422.* The classic Creole restaurant, where oysters Rockefeller was invented, run by the fifth generation of the same family. Souffléed potatoes are legendary. Amazing wine cellar. Closed Sunday.

Bacco ✪✪✪ *310 Chartres Street, New Orleans; tel. 522-2426.* A posh Italian outpost of the Brennan family (see below) with home-made and imported pasta and other gourmet ingredients in mouth-watering combinations of flavours. They even pipe Italian language lessons into the restrooms.

Bayona ✿✿ – ✿✿✿ *430 Dauphine Street, New Orleans; tel. 525-4455.* Chef Susan Spicer's version of *nouvelle cuisine* and beyond. Relaxed atmosphere and startling combinations of flavours artistically presented. Good wine list. Reasonable smart restaurant.

Brennan's ✿✿✿ *417 Royal Street, New Orleans; tel. 525-9713.* Before "power breakfasts," there were power brunches in this elegant restaurant — eggs Benedict (Canadian bacon), eggs Sardou (with artichokes), or Creole cream cheese with fresh fruit — and satisfying lunches and dinners. The birthplace of "Bananas Foster."

Café Maspero ✿ *601 Decatur Street, New Orleans; tel. 523-6250.* A bit of informal French Quarter atmosphere in a cavernous sandwich hangout so popular it's usually jammed.

Café Pontalba ✿✿ *Chartres and St. Peter streets, New Orleans; tel. 522-1180.* With a view of Jackson Square from the ground floor of the historic Pontalba building, this busy, casual café serves Cajun specialities like shrimp *étouffée* and blackened grilled catfish.

Chart House ✿✿✿ *801 Chartres Street, New Orleans; tel. 523-2015.* Dependable steaks, prime ribs, and seafood in romantic French Quarter atmosphere.

Court of Two Sisters ✿✿✿ *613 Royal Street, New Orleans; tel. 522-7261.* Charming, romantic atmosphere lures throngs of tourists for open-air dining. Daily brunch buffet with live jazz. Traditional Creole cuisine plus classic French dishes.

Desire Oyster Bar ✿✿ *Royal Sonesta Hotel, 300 Bourbon Street, New Orleans; tel. 586-0300.* Clam chowder, fresh raw oysters, boiled shrimp, even po-boy sandwiches in this crucially located, old-fashioned oyster bar. Casual atmosphere.

New Orleans

Felix's Restaurant and Oyster Bar ✪✪ *739 Iberville Street (at Bourbon), New Orleans; tel. 522-4440.* Hectic, crowded restaurant. The place to go for all manner of seafood, with friendly service. Oyster specialists, from raw to Rockerfeller. Also Jambalaya, shrimp Creole, stuffed flounder.

G & E Courtyard Grill ✪✪✪ *1113 Decatur Street, New Orleans; tel. 528-9376.* A gushing fountain and an open grill in the courtyard set the stage for sophisticated dishes, many with Italian influences. Casual atmosphere but watch out for the bill/check.

Galatoire's ✪✪ *209 Bourbon Street, New Orleans; tel. 525-2021.* Splendid gastronomic possibilities along the most traditional Creole lines, but you have to queue to get a table in this ever-popular institution, which does not accept reservations. Open for lunch and dinner Tuesday to Sunday.

Hard Rock Café ✪ *418 North Peters, New Orleans; tel. 529-5617.* The fashionable spot for rock and roll and hamburgers, ribs, steaks, sandwiches. Lunch and dinner.

Johnny's Po-Boys ✪ *511 St. Louis Street, New Orleans; tel. 524-8129.* You'll have to give up candlelight and fancy service in this hectic dispensary of Gargantuan sandwiches including po-boys and Muffulettas. Open lunchtime only.

K-Paul's Louisiana Kitchen ✪✪✪ *416 Chartres Street, New Orleans; tel. 524-7394.* A mecca of Cajun cooking, the base of chef Paul Prudhomme. Reservations are accepted for the upstairs dining room only, so eager crowds line up to try whatever has inspired the kitchen on the day in question.

La Louisiane Restaurant ✪✪✪ *725 Iberville Street, New Orleans; tel. 523-4664.* More than a century of tradition in classic Creole cuisine, with Italian touches. Baked oysters, crawfish *étouffée*, barbecued shrimp. For dessert: bread pudding. Reservations recommended. Dress smart at dinner.

La Madeleine ✪ *547 St. Ann Street, New Orleans; tel. 568-9950.* Right on Jackson Square, self-service breakfasts, lunches, and early dinners. Wholesome sandwiches, salads, quiches, and excellent home-made bread. Wide variety of delicious coffees.

Old N'awlins Cookery ✪✪ *729 Conti Street, New Orleans; tel. 529-3663.* In an informal atmosphere you can sample attractive Cajun and Creole food — blackened fish, crawfish *étouffée*, shrimp Creole, and delicious desserts. Good service.

Palace Café ✪✪ – ✪✪✪ *605 Canal Street, New Orleans; tel. 523-1661.* Where the young execs go for *nouvelle cuisine* New Orleans-style, not to mention the overwhelming desserts. Busy bistro atmosphere on the edge of the French Quarter.

Patout's ✪✪ *501 Bourbon Street, New Orleans; tel. 529-4256.* Founded in 1913 and not to be confused with Alex Patout's (see page 137), another family enterprise. Among the piquant specialities: grilled fish topped with a honey mustard beurre blanc sauce, and a crab-and-shrimp stew.

Pelican Restaurant and Bar ✪✪✪ *312 Exchange Alley (at Bienville Street), New Orleans; tel. 523-1504.* A romantic atmosphere for you to taste the carefully prepared regional specialities. Casual atmosphere, but reasonably smart. Dinner only.

Petunias ✪✪ *817 Rue St. Louis, New Orleans; tel. 522-6440.* Novel ideas for breakfast, lunch, and dinner in the shape of the "world's largest crêpes," white cloud omelet, crawfish *étouffée*, po-boy sandwiches.

Poppy's Grill ✪ *717 St. Peter Street, New Orleans; tel. 525-6724.* Breakfast 24 hours a day in this shiny diner, plus burgers and other American dishes.

Ralph & Kacoo's ✪✪ *519 Toulouse Street, New Orleans; tel. 522-5226.* Crowded, ever-popular seafood house with nautical atmosphere, big enough to offer fresh everything from oysters to trout. Noted for its "hush puppies," a flavourful deep-fried corn-bread. No reservations so be prepared to wait.

Rib Room ✪✪✪ *Omni Royal Orleans Hotel, 621 St. Louis Street, New Orleans; tel. 529-7045.* An open grill produces prime rib, roast rack of lamb, and seafood in a charming atmos-phere in the heart of the French Quarter. Dress smart.

Riverview Restaurant ✪✪✪ *Marriott Hotel, 555 Canal Street, New Orleans; tel. 581-1000.* Skyscraper view of the Mississippi, the French Quarter, and the CBD from the 41st floor. Jazz brunch on Sunday.

Samurai ✪✪ *609 Decatur Street, New Orleans; tel. 525-9595.* Among the Cajun and Creole eateries is this authentic, friendly Japanese restaurant. Sushi bar and combination dinners, sea-weed and *sukiyaki*, sake and Japanese beer.

Tony Moran's ✪ – ✪✪✪ *240 Bourbon Street, New Orleans; tel. 523-3181.* Of all things, elaborate Italian recipes in a gra-cious, historic Vieux Carré ambiance. Calimari, canneloni, carni . . . and much more, stylishly produced. There's an inexpensive pasta bistro on the ground floor.

Tujague's ✪✪ *823 Decatur Street, New Orleans; tel. 525-8676.* Established 1856, opposite the French Market, a popular, casual spot for fixed-price dinners. House speciality: brisket of beef with Creole sauce.

Vera Cruz ✪ *1141 Decatur Street, New Orleans; tel. 561-8081.* Mexican escapism — burritos, fajitas, taquitos. Closed Monday and Tuesday.

ELSEWHERE AROUND TOWN

Atchafalaya Café ✪ *901 Louisiana Avenue, Uptown, New Orleans; tel. 891-5271.* Dixieland cooking with a Creole accent — more subtle than you may imagine. No alcohol, no credit cards.

Bagel Works ✪ *132 Carondelet, CBD, New Orleans; tel. 523-7701.* Breakfast and lunch Monday to Friday featuring avocado sandwiches, gazpacho, and bagels.

Brigtsen's ✪✪ *723 Dante Street, Uptown, New Orleans; tel. 861-7610.* Rich variety of Cajun-Creole delicacies highly regarded by local aficionados. Reservations essential. Closed Sunday and Monday.

Bruning's ✪✪ *1924 West End Parkway, Lakefront, New Orleans; tel. 282-9395.* A view of the vastness of Lake Pontchartrain to enhance the seafood specialities.

Camellia Grill ✪✪✪ *626 South Carrollton Avenue, Riverbend, New Orleans; tel. 866-9573.* All-American diner for waffles, burgers, chili, and famous pecan pie. Open breakfast until 1 or 2am.

Clancy's ✪✪✪ *6100 Annunciation Street, Uptown, New Orleans; tel. 895-1111.* Near Audubon Zoo, offering imaginative recipes: rabbit sausage en croute, chicken breast in lime butter. Closed Monday and Saturday lunch, and Sunday. Casual dress. You should reserve.

Commander's Palace ✪✪✪ *1403 Washington Avenue, Garden District, New Orleans; tel. 899-8221.* This festive citadel of the Brennan family's restaurant empire (see page 136) makes the most of its stately surroundings, fresh ingredients, and the potential of Creole cuisine. Delightful views from some tables. The Creole bouillabaisse is not to be missed.

Crescent City Steak House ✪✪ – ✪✪✪ *1001 North Broad Street, Mid-City, New Orleans; tel. 821-3271.* Essentially steak, more steak, and nothing but steak — satisfying enough to have kept this institution sizzling since 1934. Closed Monday.

Emeril's ✪✪✪ *800 Tchoupitoulas Street, Warehouse District, New Orleans; tel. 528-9393.* In a large, converted factory try avant-garde Creole and American cuisine, highly praised by local gourmets for the imaginative combinations of flavours. Closed Saturday lunchtime and Sunday.

Gautreau's ✪✪✪ *1728 Soniat Street, Uptown, New Orleans; tel. 899-7397.* Small, neighbourhood-style Creole restaurant for gourmets, the surprising successor to a drugstore. Closed Sunday.

Grill Room ✪✪✪ *Windsor Court Hotel, 300 Gravier Street, CBD, New Orleans; tel. 522-1992.* Highly acclaimed breakfast, lunch, and dinner are expertly dished up among works of art in the splendid decor of what may well be the city's best hotel. Dressy. Reservations recommended.

La Gauloise ✪✪ – ✪✪✪ *Le Meridien Hotel, 614 Canal Street, CBD, New Orleans; tel. 527-6712.* A French-style bistro on the lobby level of the French-run hotel. Live jazz accompanies Sunday brunch.

Mother's ✪ *401 Poydras Street, CBD, New Orleans; tel. 523-9656.* Breakfast, lunch, dinner Creole and Cajun style, featuring baked ham, jambalaya, and po-boy sandwiches. Open daily.

Mulate's ✪✪ *201 Julia Street, Warehouse District, New Orleans; tel. 522-1492.* Modestly proclaiming to be "the world's most famous Cajun restaurant," this institution features live Cajun music to match the food — from blackened prime rib and frogs' legs to catfish in crawfish *étouffée* sauce and Zydeco gumbo (chicken, shrimp, sausage, and okra).

Pascal's Manale ✪✪✪ *1838 Napoleon Avenue, Uptown, New Orleans; tel. 895-4877.* Traditional family restaurant since

1913, seafood specialists, famous across the city for barbecued jumbo shrimp. For starters try the *remoulade* with shrimp and crabmeat. Atmosphere is crowded and congenial. Closed lunchtime at weekends.

Praline Connection ✪ *542 Frenchmen Street, Faubourg Marigny, New Orleans; tel. 943-3934.* Locals flock to this inexpensive restaurant for "soul food" of the Deep South — smothered chicken, black-eyed peas, cornbread, and sweet-potato pie.

Ruth's Chris Steak House ✪✪✪ *711 North Broad Street, Mid-City, New Orleans; tel. 486-0810.* If your diet allows only one steak, this is certainly the place to come to savour genuine U.S. prime beef, charcoal broiled — choose from the range of filet mignon, sirloin, etc., all served with shoestring potatoes. For cholesterol counters there are also excellent seafood dishes. Reservations strongly recommended.

Sazerac ✪✪✪ *Fairmont Hotel, 123 Baronne Street, CBD, New Orleans; tel. 529-4733.* Memorably elegant decor and cuisine to match, from French lobster bisque to Creole red snapper. Closed lunchtime at weekends. The name of the restaurant recalls another famous New Orleans tradition: the cocktail.

Upperline Restaurant ✪✪ *1413 Upperline, Uptown, New Orleans; tel. 891-9822.* A contemporary version of Creole cuisine, varied and adventurous, much favoured by locals. Baked oysters, quail with jambalaya, roast duck. Artistic decor. Dinner only. Reservations recommended. Closed Tuesday.

Versailles ✪✪✪ *2100 St. Charles Avenue, Uptown, New Orleans; tel. 524-2535.* In charming and elegant surroundings, Continental cuisine is complemented by Creole innovations to produce bouillabaisse, duckling *andalouse,* and veal Versailles. Elegant dress required. Dinner only. Closed Sunday.

ABOUT BERLITZ

In 1878 Professor Maximilian Berlitz had a revolutionary idea about making language learning accessible and enjoyable. One hundred and twenty years later these same principles are still successfully at work.

For language instruction, translation and inter-pretation services, cross-cultural training, study abroad programs, and an array of publishing products and additional services, visit any one of our more than 350 Berlitz Centers in over 40 countries.

Please consult your local telephone directory for the Berlitz Center nearest you or visit our web site at http://www.berlitz.com.

Helping the World Communicate